THE RISE OF URBAN AMERICA

THE
SETTLEMENT IDEA

Arthur C. Holden

ARNO PRESS
&
The New York Times

NEW YORK · 1970

206663

Reprint Edition 1970 by Arno Press Inc.

Reprinted from a copy in The University of Illinois Library

LC# 70-112549
ISBN 0-405-02455-X

THE RISE OF URBAN AMERICA
ISBN for complete set 0-405-02430-4

Manufactured in the United States of America

THE SETTLEMENT IDEA
A VISION OF SOCIAL JUSTICE

THE MACMILLAN COMPANY
NEW YORK · BOSTON · CHICAGO · DALLAS
ATLANTA · SAN FRANCISCO

MACMILLAN & CO., Limited
LONDON · BOMBAY · CALCUTTA
MELBOURNE

THE MACMILLAN CO. OF CANADA, Ltd.
TORONTO

THE
SETTLEMENT IDEA
A VISION OF SOCIAL JUSTICE

BY

ARTHUR C. HOLDEN
FORMERLY SECRETARY PRINCETON COMMITTEE
ON SOCIAL SERVICE

New York
THE MACMILLAN COMPANY
1922

CONTENTS

¶

PAGE

Introductory Note xxiii

CHAPTER I

RADICAL VS. CONSERVATIVE

1. All human beings alike require the satisfaction of .certain needs 1
2. Defence against external aggression has absorbed the first consideration of governments 1
3. Nevertheless governments must principally take thought to secure justice between man and man 2
4. Thomas Jefferson's warning 2
5. It is at length recognized that disputes between nations must cease.............. 3
6. Radical as opposed to conservative thought 3
7. The conservative as the opportunist who acts independent of any thought of social consequences 3
8. The radical as the critic and propagandist.. 4
9. Social factors are constantly changing, putting radical propaganda out of date and bringing about change in spite of the resistance of conservatives 5
10. The background of radical thought is little understood 5
11. Radical intrigue and agitation........... 7

¶   **PAGE**

12. Obligation to defend property rights puts the state behind the conservative element sometimes to the abridgment of other rights   8

13. The Russian "Red" does not understand American institutions nor does the American understand the "Red"   8

14. The average man's life is too circumscribed for him to form correct judgments, this book will attempt to point out a method for "getting an understanding"   9

CHAPTER II

THE IDEAS OF THE FOUNDERS

1. The social settlement a method of approach to social problems, which is often misunderstood   11

2. Influence of English workers.............   11

3. Canon Barnett's idea and Arnold Toynbee as a type   12

4. Founding of Toynbee Hall in 1884.......   12

5. Original statement of purposes   13

6. Canon Barnett's estimate of value of the idea   14

7. Founding of first settlement in America, 1887 ....,.............   14

8. Early aims of the movement in New York   15

9. Seth Low's estimate of its value.........   16

10. Second settlement in America founded....   17

11. The establishment of Hull House in Chicago, 1889   17

¶   PAGE

12. Miss Addams' analysis of motives in settle-
    ment work   18

13. The success of the settlement idea. Jacob
    Riis, Richard Watson Gilder, and Theo-
    dore Roosevelt early figures in the "reform
    movement" in New York   19

CHAPTER III

THE INDUSTRIAL COMMUNITY

1. The rapid growth of the industrial town and
   the changed status of the workman.......   21

2. The decline in wages   21

3. Individual workman of Colonial days his
   own master   22

4. Growth of the shop employing journeymen,
   followed by the development of the merchant   23

5. Relation of machinery to industrial development   24

6. Transition from craftsman to factory system
   of production. Immigrant competition with
   labor   25

7. Family and child labor. The plight of both
   skilled and common labor..............   26

8. Protests in America against the social degradation of the workingman   27

9. The protest in England. The Christian socialists and the Owenites   28

10. The revolt in France   29

¶ PAGE

11. The scientific socialists of Germany....... 29

12. The intellectual protest in Russia, the novelists 30

13. Contrast between the proposals of the socialists and the method of Canon Barnett..... 30

14. The intellectual awakening of today offers an
opportunity for further development of the
settlement idea 32

CHAPTER IV

FIRST CONTACT WITH THE SETTLEMENT

1. Contrast between the tenement district and
the business part of a great city.......... 33

2. New York's "East Side" 33

3. Appearance of a settlement house......... 34

4. First impression likely to be distorted...... 34

5. Table talk as an index of the spirit of the
residents' household 35

6. Impressions from contact with the average
activities of the settlement 36

7. Settlement's greatest value not evident without careful analysis 38

8. Two different classes of people come together
in the settlement 38

9. The immediate benefits are the result of what
those who have had greater advantages are
able to do for those whose opportunity has
been limited 39

10. Very few share in these immediate benefits. 39

¶   PAGE
11. Immediate benefits difficult to tabulate   40
12. Settlement renders service to individuals,
    families, the neighborhood, the city, and the
    state   40
13. Varieties and classes of individuals   41
14. The club a typical unit of individuals   41
15. Individuals come to the settlement seeking
    primarily recreation and education   42
16. The average family seeks relief on account
    of health, financial distress or conduct   42
17. Demands upon settlement by individuals and
    families are not peculiar to the settlement
    alone   42
18. Importance of point of view in any attempt
    to satisfy a social need   43
19. Settlements' appreciation of different view-
    points   44
20. Recapitulation of points of view   45

CHAPTER V

IMMEDIATE DEMANDS AND METHODS OF WORK

1. Subdivisions of settlement activities   47
2. Regular work and standardization   48
3. Extension work   48
4. Recreation work principal among regular
   activities   50
5. Recreation as a human need   50
6. Settlement must supply something more than
   recreation   51
7. The settlement and music   52

¶ PAGE

8. Art and its meaning...................... 52
9. Dramatic work 53
10. The settlement as a developer of self-expression and neighborhood expression........ 55
11. The settlement as an agency for securing accurate information as to existing social conditions 55
12. Public recreation and social centers....... 56
13. The Social Unit and the Community Council 57
14. Settlement must be prepared to answer calls for financial distress 58
15. "Organized Charity" and financial distress. 58
16. Case Work 59
17. Emergency relief in cases of acute distress must be given but should not be made an end of settlement work 59
18. Visiting nurse service of Henry Street Settlement 60
19. Responsibility for a neighborhood health program devolves upon the resident nurse in the settlement 61
20. Co-operation with the Day Nursery...... 62
21. The settlement as adviser in cases arising from conduct 62
22. Co-operation with Big Brother Movement, Juvenile Protective Association, Legal Aid Society, and other organizations.......... 63

CHAPTER VI

THE CLUB AND THE SUMMER CAMP IN SETTLEMENT WORK

¶ PAGE

1. The Club a practical working unit......... 64
2. The settlement's responsibility 64
3. The club leader 65
4. Value of the volunteer leader and necessity for popularizing an understanding of his position 65
5. Value of example in leadership.......... 67
6. The winning of the boy 69
7. The awakening of the boy 69
8. Method in club work cannot be uniform; club set standards 20
9. Critics of the club are prone to expect too much of it 20
10. The specialized Boy's Club, possibility of co-operation with the settlements 71
11. The Boy Scouts of America 72
12. Immediate relation of the camp to the settlement 73
13. Points of difference and special advantages 74
14. The camp as a democratic society 76

CHAPTER VII

REAL OR PERMANENT BENEFITS

1. The settlement is convinced that ideal democracy is possible 77

¶   PAGE

2. Modern education neglects to give the individual an understanding of his relation to
society 77

3. As opposed to salvation of the individual
soul, today we have begun to concern ourselves with social evangelism 78

4. Permanent work for the settlement as a
means of approach to a better understanding
between the elements of society.......... 79

5. Classification of society—The Social Quadrant 79

6. The line of advantages or privileges, a material division 81

7. The line of understanding, a spiritual distinction 82

8. The "social conscience" and "social responsibility".......... 82

9. Friendships made possible by the settlement   84

10. Necessity for a human understanding and a
natural social relation between those economically related to one another.......... 85

11. Opportunity for men who desire to play not
only a part but a useful part in society..... 86

12. Opportunity to put life to the test........ 87

13. The settlement does not seek to put any
theory into practice 87

14. The awakening to a consciousness of social
injustice produces at first blind rage and the
concept of the "class war".............. 88

¶ PAGE

15. The "evolutionary socialists" as opposed to the revolutionary school 88
16. Liberal reforms—the feminist movement, the labor movement 89
17. Value of social contacts of the settlement to the labor leader—the concept of the battle of understanding with unreasoning personal greed 89
18. The awakening of barren lives to social consciousness. The possibility of social justice through understanding of social values.... 91

CHAPTER VIII

SETTLEMENT ADMINISTRATION AND SUPPORT

1. Necessity for a sound fiscal basis......... 93
2. Disadvantages of an endowment policy.... 93
3. Heavy burden upon individual subscribers merely to maintain a standard.......... 94
4. The immediate neighborhood as contributors 94
5. The responsibility rests not on the neighborhood but upon society as a whole......... 95
6. The municipality not the ideal source of support though it should maintain organized social work 95
7. Industry not in a position to support the settlement 96
8. Necessity of voluntary financial support, the funds administered by trustees 97
9. The board of managers 98
10. The danger of reaction................. 98

¶		PAGE
11.	The headworker	100
12.	Types of workers, professional and volunteer	100
13.	Democratic help of Club's Council	101
14.	The budget	103

CHAPTER IX

PROBLEMS OF RACE

1.	European immigration as a source of labor supply	109
2.	Proportion of foreign born to whole population of the United States	109
3.	The American's attitude toward immigration	110
4.	The immigrant's arrival in America—living conditions in New York	110
5.	The foreign born quarter in the western city	111
6.	The native born's contempt for the foreigner, "Americanization"	112
7.	The children have the greater opportunity to learn English	114
8.	Difficulties in the way of the parent's learning the new language	114
9.	The settlement as an interpreter of America to the immigrant	115
10.	The use of the immigrant's own tongue to teach him about his new country	116
11.	Co-operation with the organized work of foreign language groups	117
12.	The contribution of the foreigner to American life	118

¶ PAGE

13. American farming has benefited especially by German and Scandinavian immigration.. 119

14. The foreigner's contribution to the arts, literature, music, and the handicrafts......... 120

15. The settlement's opportunity to stimulate the immigrant to give America his best...... 121

16. Parents not so quick as their children to grasp new ways and methods............ 121

17. Liberty is not license, it should be balanced with substance 122

18. The immigrant's contact with native American labor 123

19. The "disinterested" policy of the American employer 124

20. The padrone system 125

21. The company town and the ban on "agitators" of whatever type.................. 126

22. Necessity for understanding the employer's point of view 127

23. The tendency for racial animosities to die out in America....................... 127

24. The traditional conception in the mind of the immigrant of the democracy of the United States 128

25. Community of purpose, social ties stronger than loyalty to race, the United States as a social entity 128

26. Loyalty of naturalized Americans in the war significant of power of a nation organized upon social rather than racial lives....... 129

¶   PAGE

27. Conclusions, the foreigner must be helped
    and urged to make his contribution to Amer-
    ican life 130

CHAPTER X

PROBLEMS OF RELIGION

1. Differences in religion give rise to many
   problems which are difficult to handle.... 132
2. Settlements furnish a non-sectarian meeting
   ground for all elements in their neighborhood 132
3. Emphasis of the settlement is put upon living
   rather than teaching morals 133
4. Necessity for an outlet for religious emotions 135
5. The settlement has been compelled to disregard petty differences and go to essentials.. 135
6. Common heritage of Jew and Gentile, the
   ethical interest shown by the Jew in the
   teachings of Christ 136
7. The spirit of the settlement movement is essentially Christian 137
8. Historical Digression—The place of Socrates
   and Plato in Greek philosophy, growth of the
   humanizing influence of the Roman School 138
9. The educational contribution of the Cynics
   and Rhetoricans. The emphasis of the Pythagorean school upon personal holiness..... 139
10. Contact with the East—The rise of the
    Alexandrian school—Neo Platonism and

¶ PAGE

contact with Hebrew thought, Philo of Alexandria 139

11. The coming of Christ—His teachings represent the flowering of the philosophical thought of the time 140

12. Many of the mystical forms and superstitions of the day were appropriated by Christianity 141

13. Emphasis laid by the early church upon life in the hereafter 141

14. Definite conformities, required by the early church, insisted upon even after the Reformation. Controversy over dogma has obscured the essential religion............ 142

15. Christ showed a way of life. The end as the social good. The settlement idea as a method of living 143

CHAPTER XI

THE SETTLEMENT AND EDUCATION

1. Definition of education................. 145

2. Natural contacts, shared experience....... 145

3. Manners, tastes, preferences, esthetics—attraction and revulsion 146

4. The school as a type of artificial contact with the experience of the race—The primary and secondary task of the school............. 147

5. The pupil learns from the lesson to do what he is taught. The student learns from study to understand 148

¶   PAGE
6. The school as a democracy of natural con-
    tacts 149
7. The student is the exceptional product. The
    student as a leader 149
8. The average product of the schools has mas-
    tered the lesson only, which he fails to relate
    to life as a whole 150
9. Democratic spirit in the schools undirected 150
10. Need for a new vision in education...... 151
11. The private tutor. The unlimited influence
    of his personality and his philosophy...... 151
12. The greater possibility of control over the
    influence of the teacher, the fear of early
    independence for the child's mind........ 152
13. The value of giving the child an understand-
    ing of social needs as opposed to holding
    him under terror of discipline 152
14. The perversion of recorded history by prud-
    ish conceits and propaganda 153
15. The general opposition on the part of con-
    trolling factions to the disturbance of estab-
    lished thought and practice by the introduc-
    tion of new ideas 154
16. Our schools fulfill the task which is set them,
    the mastery of the lesson 154
17. Is the school to develop an understanding of
    social forces or is another organization to
    develop beside it? 155
18. The settlement can supplement the school and
    broaden the narrow environment of the home 156

PAGE

¶

19. The settlement can add vitality and meaning to the lives of educated people............ 157

20. The recent awakening to the idea of social values of the Y. W. C. A. 157

21. The awakening of the church. The Interchurch Report on the Steel Strike of 1919.. 158

22. The shortcomings of the school due in great measure to the shortcomings of other social factors. The settlement must not fail to fulfill its part 158

CHAPTER XII

PROBLEMS AND PITFALLS

1. Humility and openness of mind a prerequisite of the worker who would learn to understand life 160

2. Ineffective sentimentalism and confusion of mind a result of too narrow a background 160

3. The tendency of the worker to become partisan and narrow 161

4. The analogy of society and the animal organism 161

5. The society which supports its brain workers for its service also supports the parasite... 162

6. The social worker surrounded daily by poverty falls into the way of taking sides..... 162

7. Workers often the victim of association with their intellectual inferiors 163

8. Necessity for retaining outside contacts... 164

¶   PAGE

9. The resident worker must get proper recreation to keep the joy of living fresh within him 164

10. Present low economic reward. In the ideal there should be few salaried positions for which the pay should be adequate........ 164

11. Personal enthusiasms tend to carry the worker too far in one direction........... 165

12. The danger of a cheap veneer of culture.... 165

13. Where the imagination and the esthetic sense are aroused the emphasis must not be misplaced so as to make life seem too unreal.. 166

14. How far in recreation? 167

15. Co-operation with existing agencies of recreation 167

16. Danger of psychological enthusiasms wrongly used 168

                                      PAGE

17. The settlements' purpose not to reform or to uplift but to understand 168

CHAPTER XIII

HOW IS IT TO CARRY ON?

1. The settlement not a panacea 170

2. So long as a neighborhood needs friends the settlement must be on hand ready to introduce them 170

3. The test of a settlement lies not in its physical equipment but in its spirit 171

4. The neighborhood spirit 172

¶ PAGE

5. Knowledge of conditions essential 173
6. Estimate of Canon Barnett's method 173
7. The method and teaching of the economists and the socialists 174
8. Socio-economic thought 176
9. Social justice possible only through complete social understanding 176
10. Motive in the choice of a neighborhood.... 177
11. Difficulties in the way of getting into touch with neighbors 178
12. The assistance of the settlement house. Need of more living quarters and of more settlers 178
13. Labor movement unconnected with the settlement. A vital force lacking in the collective life of the organized neighborhood....... 179
14. The settlement not a panacea but a method of approach. Social relations must be understood before they can be improved. The necessity for popularizing the idea........ 180

APPENDICES

A. Statements of Settlements' Purpose by the United Neighborhood Houses of New York 182
B. The Great War and the Foreign Born Population of the United States.............. 190
C. Illiteracy and Inability to speak English in the United States 197
E. Financial Reports and Finances.......... 201
    Bibliography 207

INTRODUCTORY NOTE

Some of the deep problems of life, the perplexities, the social frictions, the regretable unfairnesses, it is not easy to understand. There are many thoughtful people who would gladly so order their lives that the whole direction of their living might be consistent with the public good, had they but positive knowledge of what that direction should be. Such knowledge cannot come until the great majority of men begin to think in social terms. Perhaps that day is still far off. Nothing, however, can help so much to bring it nearer as a conscious striving for an understanding of social conditions, social values, and social phenomena.

Among college men and women there has been a growing tendency to test out values and to ask questions. It fell to my lot shortly after graduation to become one of a committee to urge men as they came out of the colleges to take an active interest in civic and social problems. Working at such a task, it became increasingly difficult to tell the younger men just what it was for which we were soliciting their interest. It was with difficulty that our committee overcame the "holier than thou" imputation, with which we were constantly embarrassed. Even the use of the term "social service" appeared to be a stumbling block. The committee, of which I speak, came under

the influence of the settlement movement at the very
outset. Through the entrée which this contact gave
us, it was possible to make an intelligent approach to
the whole social question. The relation which the
settlement bears to our work, and indeed to any
organized piece of social work, is still, however, very
imperfectly understood. What it is all about, must
be explained anew to almost every prospective friend
who is approached.

Believing that the settlement plays an essential role,
which is of fundamental importance to society as a
whole and of vital interest to each and every human
being, whether he imagines himself to be interested
or not, I have set myself the task of interpreting the
settlement idea. Those better qualified than I to speak
have already written fluently and ably upon the subject. In a sense, it is an unwarranted assumption that
I, an architect by profession, should invade the field
of socio-economic writing. As a professional man,
however, I know that the greatest professional accomplishments are achieved for a public that demands
achievement. In general the public is rather prone to
leave the thinking about social things to the professional social worker, just as it is accustomed to leave
the field of artistic thought to artists, of religious
thought to ministers, of educational thought to professors, and to leave the care of the public health to
doctors. This shifting of responsibility is generally
accompanied by a neglect to take an interest at all and
is one of the chief reasons that our health standards
are still needlessly low, that our educational system
is antiquated, that our churches are unpopular, that

our real artists are few, and that our social system is needlessly muddled.

There has been a great deal of criticism lately of that prolific writer, Mr. H. G. Wells. He has been accused of trying to tell everybody how to run everybody else's business besides the world in general. What he really has been saying is that the world is headed for trouble unless we revise our way of thinking about things. What one man does, affects not only himself but many others. It *is* everybody's business not only what men are doing but how they are doing it. Mr. Wells has seen the need of an intellectual Renaissance, the quickening of the minds of *all* men to an interest in *all* fields of human endeavor. Our scientists, our ministers, our thinkers can not go forward without this popular support. There is a particular need for examining the organization of society, and of understanding its faults, its misplacements, and its good features. Through the settlement idea there is the opening for an approach toward a popular understanding of social problems and relationships. In this volume I have focused upon the settlement solely in the hope of popularizing it and of using it for a larger social end than it serves at present.

After all, social problems are not merely the concern of a little group of over-conscientious thinkers; if we are to progress, the great body of men and women must be stimulated to think clearly upon the subject and to demand clear thinking from their social leaders. "The great majority of men and women, in ordinary times, pass through life without ever contemplating or criticising, as a whole, either their own conditions or those of the world at large. They find themselves born into a certain place in society, and they accept what each day brings forth, without any effort of thought beyond what the immediate present requires. Almost as instinctively as the beasts of the field, they seek the satisfaction of the needs of the moment, without much forethought, and without considering that by sufficient effort the whole conditions of their lives could be changed. A certain percentage, guided by personal ambition, make the effort of thought and will which is necessary to place themselves among the more fortunate members of the community; but very few among these are seriously concerned to secure for all the advantages which they seek for themselves. It is only a few rare and exceptional men who have that kind of love toward mankind at large that make them unable to endure patiently the general mass of evil and suffering, regardless of any relation it may have to their own lives." [1]

The following pages could never have been put into the form in which they are, had it not been for the untiring support of certain good friends, who were wise enough to condemn manuscript unsparingly and unselfish enough to give valuable time and suggestion towards its revision. For the original thought that prompted me to undertake the book, I am indebted to Professor V. G. Simkhovitch. Those whom I desire principally to thank for criticism and suggestion are: Ferdinand D. Sanford, Franklin C. Wells, Jr., George Alexander Armstrong, Tertius van Dyke, Curtiss

---

[1] Bertrand Russell. "Proposed Roads to Freedom."

Wheeler, Edward Hale Bierstadt, and Viola P. Conklin. Severest and most penetrating of all critics, my wife deserves the especial gratitude of the reader for her discerning insistence on revision.

ARTHUR C. HOLDEN.

New York, June, 1921.

THE SETTLEMENT IDEA

CHAPTER I

RADICAL VERSUS CONSERVATIVE

1. Human beings, whether refined by training or not, have within them the germinals of the same needs, motives, impulses, and desires. It is not possible for life to go on unless certain of the most fundamental human needs are satisfied. All men alike require food and drink, exercise and rest, shelter, and occupation for the mind, and an outlet for the faculties of sex. Democratic governments are maintained to insure to all men the "right to life, liberty and the pursuit of happiness."

2. In the earliest tribal development, it was the patriarch who meted out justice among his followers. As time went on, however, a newer and different responsibility was placed upon the leader of the tribe. It became his duty to protect the society of his own people against external aggression. In the attempt to shatter the menacing power of an unfriendly state, war came into the world. The modern state has concentrated upon equipment to defend itself against external aggression but it has not been uniformly capable of maintaining all of its constituent members in the enjoyment of their natural rights. In the appalling struggles that have taken place between nations, the primitive social functions of the state have been often lost

1

sight of and the state organization developed and improved with the primary purpose of assuring the stability of the organization itself.

3.   Nevertheless the struggle for the maintenance of essential right between man and man has been always going on.   Occasionally it has been marked by great outbursts and convulsions which have threatened the stability of the social order itself.   The French Revolution shook Europe to its foundations. On our own continent the American Revolution took a somewhat different form.   The necessity was recognized and the attempt was made to set up an ideal form of government.   There was no passion for revenge upon a particular class such as unbalanced the revolutionary leaders of France.

4.   It had come to be recognized that men are dominated by motives which tend to control their actions beyond the enjoyment of their elemental needs. Motives such as the love of praise, the love of possession and the love of controlling, lead some to acquire power greater than obtainable by most men.   The restraint which government exercises is applied to protect men from those whose own ambitions lead them to neglect consideration of their fellows.   In drawing up the Federal Constitution, Americans recognized the necessity for specific guarantees of liberty.   Thomas Jefferson spoke out fearlessly upon this subject:

"The spirit of the time may alter, will alter. Our rulers will become corrupt, our people careless.   A single zealot may become persecutor and better men become his victims.   It can never be too often repeated that the time for fixing essential right, on a legal basis, is while our rulers are honest, ourselves united. From the conclusion of this war we shall be going down hill. It will not then be necessary to resort every moment to the people for support. They will be forgotten, therefore, and their rights disregarded. They will forget themselves in the sole faculty of making money, and will never think of uniting to effect a due respect for their rights. The shackles, therefore, which shall not be knocked off at the conclusion of this war will be heavier and heavier, till our rights shall revive or expire in a convulsion."

5. Today we stand perhaps at the beginning of a new day. The recognition that wars between nations must cease, and the establishment of an international league to settle disputes between peoples, should lessen the troublesome burden of national defense and free the state again to turn its best energies to the maintenance of justice within its borders.

6. And now at a time when all intellectual effort should be concentrated upon interpreting the changes brought about through the war and upon understanding the new inter-relations of men, we are engaged in the old battle of the radical versus the conservative. It is a natural division between men, due perhaps to a different outlook and a different way of thinking about things in general.

7. Speaking broadly the conservative is more generally the opportunist. He is quite ready to play the game of life taking things just as he finds them and regulating his conduct only by the restraint of estab-

lished custom. He is not likely to question the social consequences of any act of his so long as it is an act permitted by common practice. His answer to the criticism of the unfortunate condition in which the majority of people live is that most men do not know what is good for them; that they have brought these conditions upon themselves; that such is the way of human life and it can never be otherwise. There are plenty of well meaning people of this type who devoutly thank God for the many blessings that they themselves have received while they offer genuine sympathy for their fellows who have not been so fortunate. There still, however, exist some who would rule their brothers with an iron hand and teach them by force what is good for them.

8. The radical in general is a man who criticizes complacency and, as the derivation of the word implies, proposes to go to the root of things for his remedy. There have been many types. They have put forward various proposals for the improvement of the social organization which have been received by conservatively minded people with uniform abhorrence. The radical, whose influence has been pre-eminent and whose proposals have received widespread consideration, was Karl Marx, the socialist. His proposals were definite, he preached revolution as the inescapable means of social readjustment. He believed that the proletariat after being forced lower and lower by the oppression of capitalism would at length revolt. The proletariat of today, however, is not the same proletariat of which Marx wrote in his great work "Das Kapital." It has changed. Although greater and greater wealth has

been concentrated in the hands of the capitalists, the laboring man has not been reduced to the abject wage slavery that was prophesied. The increase in wealth has actually given him more earning power and a larger share of income. Through his ability to organize he has been able in a measure to control wages. The proletarian revolution will not come about in the way nor for the reasons that were prophesied by Karl Marx.

9. The factors which make up the social whole are interrelated and interdependent. When a single factor changes in value the relation to the others and to the whole itself changes. Though we are accustomed to use the word revolution to describe a sudden change, changes just as revolutionary may come about by slow natural development. Programs which are put forward to remedy definite conditions lose force and value as the world marches onward and those conditions change. Conservatives are prone to be overshocked and prejudiced by the programs which are put forward and to waste their energies in useless resistance to the particular program. The course which is generally taken is suppression of the advocates of the despised doctrine, based upon their alleged transgression of established courses of conduct. What the conservative fears is social distintegration brought about by too sudden change. This resistance to ill-considered change has certainly a definite social value.

10. Among conservatives, however, there has been little understanding and little attempt to understand the background which underlies radical propaganda. They understand for example little of the history of the

Russian "Red" who, brought up under the most medieval and oppressive government that modern times has known, has become convinced that all government is oppressive and tyrannical and hypocritical. He has been aroused by various grades of radical thought, the humanitarianism of Tolstoy, the anarchism of Bakunin and Kropotkin, and the violent example of Ravachol. Before he has even realized that his own people have won what the people of other nations have long enjoyed, namely, political self-expression, he assumes that the government of other nations being like his own, which he has just overthrown, wish to oppress and exploit him again and to reinstate the oppressor and the rule of the landlord. The "Red" looks upon governments as the tool and instrument of those who have power. He does not believe in the sincerity of representative government. He comes to the United States and is thrust into crowded tenement districts where the living conditions are vile. He hears some talk about the vote, but he sees his ignorant neighbors marshalled to the polls and exploited by the ward boss whose vision includes only the establishment of the political security of his own faction and the milking of political offices for personal advantage. The "Red" concludes that in a democracy the capitalist and the landlord are as firmly intrenched as they were under the corrupt political system that he knew at home. He concludes that the capitalist and the landlord let the puppets play for their penny worth of gain so long as the system remains secure. The "Red," therefore, preaches anarchy to his "oppressed brother" in the United States as the only means that he knows of escaping from exploitation by the moneyed class.

11. Reinforcing this type of anarchistic agitator is the intriguing emissary of the Bolshevik government. He is the paid servant of a government that has gained its power by revolution, that has had to fight opposition at home and that has maintained itself by a system of hostages, execution, and confiscation. Those at the head of this revolutionary government have had a purpose which they have attempted to accomplish. Their program has been the most visionary, the most revolutionary and, in the light of past experience, the most impossible that any party in any country ever sought to accomplish. The Bolsheviki have found themselves distrusted and suspected not alone by individuals and parties but by the organized governments of the world. Their basic belief in the class war teaches them to suspect that class interests are at the root of the opposition to their program. The conviction on the part of the Bolsheviki that all governments are organized by the moneyed and landed classes for the maintenance of property rights and for the exploitation of the wage earner, teaches them to look upon all governments as their natural enemies. The paid agent of the Bolsheviki therefore works with the anarchistic idealist [2] for the overthrow of all government.

The "Reds" meet, as they did in their own country, in secret. They attempt to stir up industrial discontent. They preach "class war"! They "agitate"! The "Red" includes in his agitation advocacy of the overthrow of

---

[2] See Russell. "Proposed Roads to Freedom."

the government. Ignored at first he is finally apprehended and perhaps imprisoned. He is filled with
jealousy and rage toward the officials who have apprehended him. He is convinced that, like the imperial
police of bureaucratic Russia, all government officials
are the servants of the landed class and the capitalists.

12. On the other hand, there are enough selfish
men who would prostitute the instruments of free
government for their own selfish ends to give color
to his suspicions. The protection of property often
calls the police to take a side against men and women,
who have a just grievance. The right in law to the
defence of property rights is universally recognized,
but it has frequently been made a paramount issue
for no other reason than to obscure the existence of
other rights and to compel the state to side with property
holders. The American tendency to insist upon the letter
rather than upon the spirit of the law, has put the man
without property and without money at a great dis-
advantage and has led to discrimination against him.

13. The Russian "Red" understands American institutions as little as does the average American appreciate the pernicious oppression of the Russian Imperial
system. In fact the foreigner will laugh in the native
born American's face and tell him that he is a hypo-
crite, that his so-called free institutions are only part
of a system for the exploitation of the laboring man
and he will cite as proof positive the fact that he
himself has been apprehended by the police, his meetings broken up and his friends imprisoned.[3] There are

---

[3] See "Illegal Practices of the Department of Justice."

plenty of sincere idealists among the so-called "Reds" but they lack complete understanding. Then in addition there is a following of selfish men who see in the programs of radicals an easy way of gaining material goods and properties for their personal enjoyment which they might not otherwise obtain. There are enough of these to give color to the opinion of the free born American that the Bolsheviki are a set of hypocrites and scoundrels. But the average American lacks understanding of how or why the Bolshevik school of thought came into existence. The average American is apt also to form quick judgments and generalizations. He is likely to include in the category of "Reds" all those whose ideals and motives differ radically from his own. He fortifies himself behind the declaration that he himself is "one hundred percent American." Conservatives can only see an immediate menace to the established order in the program of the radicals. They do not seek and do not understand the motives, the desires, or the aspirations that underlie the program. On the other hand the radical can see only the policy of resistance to any change which appears to actuate conservatives, and he can attribute such a policy only to self interest.

14. The two points of view are far apart with little chance that either can be brought directly to an understanding of the other. The lives which men lead are conscripted and narrow. One's vision is limited by the small circle of contacts which are the result of every day existence. Such an experience of life, as is enjoyed by the average man, is not broad enough for him to base upon it his conception of the ideal

society toward which humanity is struggling and laboring. The purpose of this volume is to point out a very simple method of broadening the social vision and of getting an understanding of social needs. I do not lay claim to any originality. I do not intend to point to anything new. I do, however, intend to point to something that is being done but of which the real significance is appreciated only by a very few. It is my belief that, if this method of approach, which, for lack of a better name, I have called the "Settlement Idea," can be more popularly understood, it will become a common way of life and life itself may be rid thereby of many of its complexities and its misunderstandings.

CHAPTER II

1. In approaching a study of the social settlement it is of value to take a brief survey of the work of the founders of the movement. The modern settlement house has a form which bears a resemblance to other present day organizations whose purposes and methods differ greatly. Those unacquainted with these differences and unfamiliar with the ends sought are often confused and misled as to the place that the settlement really occupies in society. For this reason it is well to go back to the beginning and inquire into the original purposes and ideals of the founders.

2. In the first place, the settlement is a creation of our Anglo-Saxon race. It had its beginning in England. Early in the last century the attention of the English people had been directed to the misery of the working people by Harriet Martineau and other writers of her type. Robert Owen stood out head and shoulders among a group of reformers. Charles Kingsley lead his workingmen's clubs. John Ruskin and Thomas H. Green were influential at Oxford. Finally John R. Green and Samuel A. Barnett were the men who conceived the idea of residence among the poor of east London, and to the latter belongs

11

the credit for making the first constructive step toward the founding of the settlement.

3. A letter from him written in 1883 was instrumental in bringing several Oxford students to live in one of the poorer parts of London. The letter was in answer to a request for advice from a group who were interested in doing something for the poor. Mr. Barnett wrote: "The men might hire a house, where they could come for short or long periods and, living in an industrial quarter, learn to sup sorrow with the poor." One of this group was Arnold Toynbee. A personality at Oxford in his student days, Toynbee, made a fellow and lecturer in economics, became a powerful influence for social improvement. He made a special study of the Industrial Revolution and its effect upon the workingman, and in addition to this, he took up a vigorous campaign of platform speaking. The strain was too much for him for he died in 1883 at the age of only 31, leaving the incompleted notes for his projected book. But in spite of his early death it was Toynbee who had inspired the little group at Oxford to take an active interest in the struggles of the poor. Accordingly when Canon Barnett brought his group to live in an industrial quarter of London, and when a house was established to meet their growing needs and the desire was felt to give it a name which would be, as Mrs. Barnett put it, "free from every possible savor of a mission," it was made a memorial to Arnold Toynbee and called Toynbee Hall.

4. Toynbee Hall was founded in July, 1884, by the University Settlement Association acting as a committee for Oxford and Cambridge Universities.

Property was bought and the house refitted, with lecture and meeting rooms as well as living quarters for the residents. Canon Samuel A. Barnett, both on account of his knowledge of the district of White Chapel and the fact that his had been the original suggestion, was made the first warden. The following is from the first report of the Association:

5. "As a means whereby the thought, energy and public spirit of the University may be brought into the direct presence of the social and economic problems of our times, the value of the experiment cannot be overrated. The main difficulty of poor city neighborhoods, where the toilers who create our national prosperity are massed apart, is that they have few friends and helpers who can study and relieve their difficulties, few points of contact with the best thoughts and aspirations of their age, few educated public-spirited residents, such as elsewhere in England uphold the tone of Local Life and enforce the efficiency of Local Self-Government. In the relays of men arriving year by year from the Universities in London to study their professions or to pursue their independent interests, there are many free from the ties of later life, who might fitly choose themselves to live amongst the poor, to give up to them a portion of their lives, and endeavor to fill the social void.

"It is an enterprise, which if patiently maintained and effectually developed, cannot but beget experience which will react most practically upon the thought of the educated classes upon whom, in a democratic country, falls so deep a responsibility for local and central good government . . . . The Council lays down its work with the hope that . . . each member of the Association will do his utmost to kindle an interest in the condition of the people, amongst men as they come up to the Universities. The solution of the Social Question lies in the thought of the young men of England."

6. In his first report as warden, Canon Barnett says: "A review of our three months' life together in Toynbee Hall leaves me conscious that too much has come to our hands to do. . . . It may be well to group the occupations of the residents as Teachers, Citizens, Hosts. . . . Yet it is impossible to group all that has been done under these heads. To our visitors entertainment may have seemed to be the object to which the residents have attached the most importance. It is not so. The best work has been done more secretly, when two or three have met week by week and have learned the truth from one another."

7. In 1886 an American, Stanton Coit, went to live at Townbee Hall. The following winter Dr. Coit returned and with his friend, Charles B. Stover took up his residence in Forsythe Street on the lower East Side. Out of this experiment grew the Neighborhood Guild, founded 1887, the first social settlement in America. In 1891 the name was changed to the University Settlement and a report was issued. Refer-

ence to this report gives an insight into some of its early problems and aims. The following is from the Constitution:

> "The work of the Society calls for men who will reside in the Neighborhood House and give to the people of the neighborhood a large part of their time and services; it calls also for men and women who can give it but a small portion of their time, but who are willing to assist by taking charge of the kindergarten class, clubs for boys and girls, meetings and entertainments for men and women; it calls for subscriptions and donations from all who believe that good results can be accomplished by bringing men and women of education into closer relation with the laboring classes."

8. Speaking of Toynbee and Oxford Halls in London and of the Neighborhood Guild in New York the first report continues: "In all three institutions the ends sought have been much the same, viz., the cultivation of friendly relations between the educated and uneducated, and the gradual uplifting of the latter by the better influences thus brought to bear upon them. The Neighborhood Guild has endeavored to make its house at No. 147 Forsythe Street, the town-hall and the club-house of its particular locality—the place where the people of the neighborhood could come together for special purposes, for lectures, concerts, etc., where social clubs and educational classes could meet and it has so far succeeded that about two hundred and fifty people of the neighborhood regularly

visit the house, and one hundred more, not members of the Guild, attend lectures. The house has also served as a residence for three or four workers who have regularly visited among their neighbors, performing various kindly offices, and thus making friends among the people of the vicinity. . . . Excellent results have been accomplished and it has been demonstrated that educated men and women, living and working among the poor, associating with them as equals, but introducing into the tenement house all that trained intelligence and friendly sympathy have to give, can make themselves a most efficient means of bettering and elevating the mental, moral and physical condition of the people. . . . The experiments in London and in other foreign cities teach us much, but the great difference between the conditions in this city and in foreign cities make our social problems in a large measure different from theirs, and makes their hard-earned knowledge of only general value to us."

9. In his Report of 1894, Hon. Seth Low, President of the Society, said: "One who passes his life in the midst of refined surroundings has only to think for a moment to realize how little he knows about the life of a large part of his fellow-citizens. . . . It is equally true that the laboring man knows as little about the educated and rich people of New York as the latter knows about the laboring man. Out of this mutual ignorance is bred mutual suspicion and mutual distrust. . . . Nothing so well as knowledge based upon actual acquaintance can scatter such shadows. Everything therefore that tends to make the different classes of people that make up the citizenship of this

city better acquainted with one another is a step
toward making the life of our city better in all its
aspects. The University Settlement Society offers one
of the very best platforms of the city upon which the
employer and the laboring man can meet on equal
terms. It is not so much that other platforms do not
exist. It is rather that there are very few platforms,
as a matter of fact, to which such different types of
men are ready to go. By its services to the people
of the neighborhood the University Settlement has
obtained a hearing in the Tenth Ward. This position
of advantage should be maintained. . . . Its capacity
to be of service is limited only by its ability to command men and women who will give their personal
service to its cause and others who can supply money
necessary to make effective the machinery that can
set it in motion."

10.   Two years after the establishment of the Neighborhood Guild the College Settlement was opened on
Rivington Street, New York. This was as a field of
work for an organization of representative college
women. Some of the workers had visited the English
Settlement and others had worked with Dr. Coit.

11.   In that same year there was opened in Chicago
what was destined to become probably the most famous
social settlement in America. Miss Jane Addams
and Ellen Gates Starr established Hull House on
Halsted Street. We will let Miss Addams speak for
herself: "It is hard," she writes, "to tell just when
the simple plan which afterwards developed into the
Settlement began to form itself in my mind. It may
have been even before I went to Europe for the second

time, but I gradually became convinced that it would be a good thing to rent a house in a part of the city where many primitive and actual needs are found, in which young women who had been given over too exclusively to study, might restore a balance of activity along traditional lines and learn of life from life itself, where they might try out some of the things that had been sought and put truth to the ultimate test of the conduct it dictates or inspires."

12.   It was in 1888 that Miss Addams visited Toynbee Hall and the People's Palace in East London.   In later years, in writing of the founding of her own settlement she wrote: "It is quite impossible for me to say in what proportion or degree the subjective necessity which lead to the founding of Hull House combined the three trends: (1) the desire to interpret democracy in social terms;   (2) the impulse beating at the very source of our lives urging us to aid in race problems;   (3) the Christian movement toward humanitarianism.   It is difficult to analyze a living thing; the analysis is at best imperfect.   Many more motives may blend with the three trends; possibly the desire for a new form of social success due to the nicety of imagination which refuses worldly pleasures unmixed with the joys of self-sacrifice; possibly a love of approbation, so vast that it is not content with the treble clapping of delicate hands, but wishes also that the base notes from the toughened palms may mingle with these.   . . . The Settlement, then, is an experimental effort to aid in the solution of the social and industrial problems which are engendered by the modern conditions of life in a great city."

13. Two years after Hull House was started, a third settlement was founded in New York, East Side House in the Yorkville District. In the same year Professor William J. Tucker established Andover House, later to become known as South End House, in Boston. Robert A. Woods, just returned from studies in England, was made the head worker. The settlement movement now became well established in America. It was no longer a question of experiment, but of success, of force, of vigor and personality, and of the individual adaptability of the scores of settlements, which now sprang up to their respective localities. In all the principal cities of the country influential houses were established in the early nineties. Chicago Commons founded in 1894 by Graham Taylor, and Kingsley House in Pittsburgh deserve special mention. The reader is referred to the very excellent "Handbook of Settlements" prepared by Robert A. Woods and Albert J. Kennedy, in which is included some mention of all of the known settlement centers both in the United States and abroad.

But before passing to the discussion of the settlement as it exists today, one more figure must be mentioned. Although he will not be remembered primarily as a settlement worker, no discussion of the launching of the movement in America would be complete without mention of the name of the late Jacob A. Riis. As he himself stated a short time before his death, he had found that he had a pen and a tongue and he used them in bringing home to the nation a knowledge of living conditions in industrial quarters. His books popularized the subject. He was notably the educator of the early reform movement in New York, though his work was not confined to the city alone. He exerted a far reaching influence over the new generation by his lectures at schools and colleges. It was Jacob Riis' contention that the "Slum" had been abolished. Certain it is, that crowded and filthy as the tenement districts of our large cities still are, they are not the "slums" which disgraced our civilization in the closing quarter of the last century. The name of Richard Watson Gilder of New York is another which will long be remembered as one of the greatest influences for good in the battle of the eighties and nineties against unwholesome living conditions. The vigorous personality of the youthful Theodore Roosevelt, who was at that time the city's police commissioner, was a powerful influence in sustaining the work of Riis and Gilder.

CHAPTER III

1.   In the mushroom industrial cities of a world, whose imagination was being fired by the newly revealed potentialities of machinery, conditions had arisen, never experienced before, which were bringing about misadjustments in the social system, with which neither the moral nor the intellectual capacities of the community were able to cope. In England particularly, the flow of the population to the cities was so rapid and so out of proportion to the capacity of the manufactories and collieries to absorb the "hands" that the very greatest suffering was unavoidable and a distinct lowering of the standards of living resulted. The increased use of labor saving devices which was the stimulus for the increase in manufacturing and the consequent growth of the city, was also the cause of the decrease in the value of individual hand labor. The plight of the low grade unskilled workman therefore became worse and worse until he was forced into a condition of abject poverty and "wage slavery."

2.   As the immediate result of the introduction of machinery, the market value of labor had fallen so low that society was powerless economically to care for its lower strata.   The lowest grade of worker was unable to maintain himself upon the wages paid

21

even if he labored all of the time, and it must be remembered that he could not work all of the time but only when his employers needed his assistance.   It is hard writing in this day of after war high wages to appreciate the plight of the industrial worker of a hundred years ago.[*]   It is difficult even to think back over the last twenty or thirty years and realize the hopelessness of the wage earner's situation as it appeared then. I can do no more here than to attempt briefly to sketch the character of the economic changes of the so-called Industrial Revolution of the Eighteenth and Nineteenth Centuries.   For a better understanding of the subject as well as of contemporary thought which has sought to remedy existing evils I must refer the reader to the special bibliography at the end of the volume which has been prepared to assist in the study of social conditions.

3.   Let us picture to ourselves first a typical development in one of the industries of our country.   In early Colonial times the itinerant bootmaker went from home to home working upon shoes which he made from the leather that was supplied him.   There is the record of an early charter issued to the shoemakers of Boston in 1648 which was modeled on the British guilds of that day, which states that the shoemaker established in his own shop shall not "refuse to make shoes for any inhabitant at reasonable rates of their owne leather." We find that the craftsmen now in possession of his

---

[*] Since this writing a wage decline has set in.   Again there is the problem of unemployment.   Considered in its relation to purchasing power undoubtedly the position of the wage earner has improved in the past one hundred years.

shop carried on what was known as "bespoke work" for special orders as well as an inferior quality of "shop work" that he might have ready to hand something with which to supply his casual customer. The early charters granted by the Colonies to special guilds were similar to the British, and gave to the trades the right to examine their craftsmen and obtain orders from the court suppressing anyone who was not "a sufficient workman."

4. As the next step in the development we find the small shopkeeper employing more journeymen and making more effort to sell his wares. We read of New England shopkeepers risking their lives in a journey by sea to southern ports, there to secure "orders at a very low figure." We find records of disputes arising from the effort of wholesalers of this type to reduce their journeymen's wages. We find here an early type of capitalist, who employed a larger number of journeymen, but who had to secure over and above the *wages* he paid a *profit* on his venture. The next stage of development we discover in the merchant capitalist. We can realize the benefit of the maintenance of a warehouse in a convenient location in the business district of the growing Colonial cities. The manufacturer, however, could not amass sufficient capital to have his own individual warehouse. We find in consequence, a merchant owning such a warehouse where the goods of many manufacturers in different branches of industry were offered for sale. This removes by still another step the maker of a pair of shoes from the consumer. Originally the maker supplied the consumer's wants directly by going

to his house and creating the article desired, taking his profit in the form of direct payment. We now find the maker receiving a wage for his labor while the product of his labor belongs to the master mechanic or manufacturer who incurs the responsibility of disposing of the product for a profit. Finally we find the manufacturer sharing a portion of his profit with the merchant for the service rendered of actually marketing the article.

5. I recite these points in the development of our industrial system because of their close relation to the change in the status of the worker. While the development was caused partly by the introduction of machinery, in a sense it was partly this development that demanded the discovery of some method for increasing production. This is especially true of the United States. It had been the policy of the original Colonies to foster and encourage manufactures. This had been done by special grants and privileges. After the Revolution, with the resumption of foreign trade, the American manufacturer found himself unable to compete with improved European methods of production. The British Parliament prohibited the exportation of tools and machinery; designs or models were not allowed to be taken out of the country. The Americans, thrown on their own resources, tried two means of surmounting the difficulty. The first was a political method, namely the imposition of a tariff on foreign goods. The second was the attempt to devise methods of their own for increasing production. In the early eighteen hundreds we find all of the guilds and trades associations offering bounties and premiums to those who

could devise "inventions and improvements in their art." With the discovery and introduction of these "improvements" which in general took the form of machinery we find a great increase in the capital investment required of the manufacturer. He was required not only to provide a place for his journeymen to work but to provide in addition the new machinery which was to make possible the increased production. Of a consequence the business had to *pay the wages* of labor, earn an *interest on capital* invested, pay a commission on marketing charges, and reward the capitalist sufficiently to *compensate him for the risk* of the enterprise.

6. This is not an account of the development of the capitalistic system. The reason that I have given this brief outline is to make clear the change that the status of the workman had undergone from the latter part of the eighteenth to the first half of the nineteenth century. It is a difficult question to understand and one which varies with the industry and with local conditions. Briefly stated the change is from the individual craftsman to the factory system of production. Was this change accompanied by a change in the social status and in the living conditions of this growing class of wage earners? Most certainly it was. We have only to call to mind the growth of our early industrial towns and to picture to ourselves again their squalor and hopelessness. We find continual records of protest in the early part of the nineteenth century on the part of labor organizations against immigration, and we find charges laid that the capitalists by seeking the cheapest labor available were

impoverishing the native sons of the country. The
European Revolutions of 1848 sent a still greater flood
of immigrants to the United States, which, suffering
from industrial depression following the panic of 1837,
was not able to assimilate the unfortunates from abroad
without materially lowering the prevailing standards
of wages and living conditions. The result was a
repetition in America of the unfortunate conditions
which the Industrial Revolution had brought about in
Europe.

7. The wage of the skilled worker began to decline as he was forced to meet the competition of the
increased supply of unskilled labor. The case of the
shoe-makers in the town of Lynn is typical. It became
impossible to support a family upon the declining wage.
As a result, other members of the family went out
to seek employment in the factory, thereby increasing
the supply of unskilled labor and bringing the average
wage down still further. The family was able to
subsist, however, upon the combined income of parents
and children and such substance as was yielded by
primitive back yard farming. The family wage thus
became the standard and the children were signed over
to the factory system. Though the evils of child labor
were far worse in England than in the United States,
the system became so firmly intrenched, that even
humane employers, honestly desirous of bettering conditions, found themselves brought face to face with
the alternative of accepting the prevailing standards
or being forced to the wall by the competition of the
more unscrupulous taskmasters.

All through the first half of the last century the

condition of the American wage earner was growing worse. The prevailing working day averaged over twelve hours. It must be remembered that the right to vote had been limited to property holders up to about 1820-1822. In 1829-30 there was an acute condition of unemployment. The files of the contemporary daily papers are loud in their appeals for help for the great numbers of skilled mechanics unable to obtain any kind of occupation. In March, 1850, the chief of police of New York City took a census of the inhabited cellars. It was found that 18,456 persons occupied 8,141 cellars with no other rooms. This meant that about one-thirtieth of the population of New York City lived underground.[5]

8. As a protest against such conditions we find the rise of a group of "idealist reformers" and writers. Robert Owen came to America to try his unsuccessful experiment at New Harmony, Indiana. America itself produced Thoreau, Emerson, Walt Whitman, Channing, Brownson, Albert Brisbane, and Horace Greeley. All kinds and descriptions of Co-operative and Mutual Aid societies sprang into existence. There were land reform associations and associations that sought the improvement of factory conditions. Besides these organizations of the intellectuals there were organizations of the laborers themselves. There were to be noted the growing frequency of strikes and the first beginnings of an organized national labor movement in the United States. It must be recalled that as the nineteenth century drew into its last quarter, the opposi-

---

[5] See Part IV, Chapter I of Commons, "History of Labor in the U. S."

tion of the interests of capital and labor seemed to be more and more sharply defined and, as labor became better and more thoroughly organized, the opposition grew into open contest and bitter dispute.

9. In England where the difficulties were even more acute than in America, the movement for reform was also widespread. Only a few years previous to the time when Canon Barnett started his settlement, the Salvation Army had issued its challenge to the world. The so-called "home mission" had also come into being. Both of these movements represented the viewpoint of men who believed that "wickedness" among the working people was responsible for their degradation. The missions and the Salvation Army set out to "save" the lower classes. Quite a different attitude was taken by another type of reformer, the so-called Christian Socialist, as represented by John Ruskin, Charles Kingsley, and William Morris. They decried the growing importance of machinery and attempted to dignify and glorify hand labor, insisting that the position of the working man was one which should not be looked down upon. Another group known as the Owenites was made up of the followers of that industrial genius Robert Owen. As a successful mill manager he was without a peer in the England of his time. Better work, he said, was the logical result of better conditions of life. He insisted that a fair portion of his phenomenal profits should be applied towards creating more favorable home environment. His program embraced both shorter working hours and better educational facilities. His especial interest, however, was the model community.

It was in this connection that he made his trip to America.

10. All over nineteenth century Europe the protest against industrial conditions was vocal. In France, Fourier put forward his version of the model community. Saint Simon wrote voluminously upon a plan for remodeling society. The influence of the writings of Rousseau in the century preceding must not be lost sight of. His was an ideal of a political state and it was this ideal that had dominated the Terror of the first Revolution. After the political collapse and reaction, the revolutionary influence of German socialism helped to keep a French revolutionary party active. It must be remembered that in the critical period 1870-71 the Communes actually established their power in Paris and maintained it for a few months.

11. In Germany itself the socialists were intellectually the dominating factor in the movement for industrial and economic reform. In 1848 Karl Marx and Frederick Engels published their "Communist Manifesto." They held that the selfishness of the "ruling classes" was the cause of the sufferings of the poor. In the words of Engels himself their doctrine was: "that the whole history of mankind (since the dissolution of primitive tribal society holding land in common ownership) has been a history of class struggles, contests between exploiting and exploited, ruling and oppressed classes; that the history of these class struggles forms a series of evolutions in which, nowadays, a stage has been reached where the exploited and the oppressed class—the proletariat—cannot attain its emancipation from the sway of the exploiting and

ruling classes—the bourgeoisie—without at the same time, and once for all, emancipating society at large from all exploitation, oppression, class distinctions and class struggles." In other words the German school of socialists which included Lassalle, Engels and Marx was actively revolutionary. They held that poverty must be abolished; that the capitalists will never permit it to be abolished because it is to their interest to obtain the cheapest labor possible and for this reason to keep a certain portion of the available labor supply near to the starvation point. Therefore, they contended, the proletariat, the workers must arise and take that wealth which they themselves have created under the lash of their exploiters.

12. Although Russia in the nineteenth century was behind the rest of Europe in industrial development, criticism of existing conditions was no less evident among the writers of the period. In Russia, however, the question which was uppermost was "land." The conflict was between landowner and serf rather than between industrial worker and manufacturer. The novelists Tolstoi, Dostoieffsky and Turgenev reflect the growth of the intellectual revolt against the sufferings entailed by the existing order of things.

13. I have briefly touched upon these various attempts at reform and particularly upon the teachings of the so-called scientific socialists of Germany, because I wished to present them to American readers in the twentieth century in the light of their historical origin. I am not subscribing to the various doctrines proclaimed. I merely desire to point out that their reason for being was the widely felt desire to relieve the

suffering of the poor whose condition had been growing steadily worse from the latter half of the eighteenth
century through the greater part of the nineteenth.

The sincerity of the work of the socialists is as
evident as the sincerity of Canon Barnett's method.
There is, however, an essential difference in funda-
mentals. The socialist doctrine is based on the anti-
pathy of class interests and the concept of the class
war. It proclaims the failure of the capitalistic system
and aims at public rather than private ownership of
property, claiming that the private owner because of
his class interest cannot be trusted. Class interest,
however, is only one form of natural human selfishness.
The socialists have the same human qualities to deal
with in the administration of public property. The
socialist hypothesis contemplates the victory of one
class over another and the abolition of the property
holding or ruling class. In reality the fact must be
faced that a new "administrative" class is substituted
for the ruling class. The same human frailties are
to be found in these new guardians of property *unless
they can be inspired by a realization of social values
so that all men are actuated solely by a desire to serve
the social body.* When socialists are faced with this
fact they come up against the first hypothesis of Canon
Barnett's method of approach. He founded his settlement believing that if men understood social conditions they would awaken to a realization of the identity
of the interests shared by what are apparently different
classes, and govern their actions so as to promote the
greatest social good. The assumption is that if men
realized the consequences of material selfishness they

would not be selfish.   To me this is the most sub-
stantial foundation stone for social reform.   It is certainly a better starting point than the assumption that
all men are so selfish that they will not change their
way of doing things unless compelled by force.

14.   It must be remembered that Canon Barnett
began his work in an atmosphere of antagonism and
distrust when comparatively few men were awake to
the need of a new outlook upon life.   Today we are
far enough from the industrial revolution to look back
and analyze the forces that were working havoc with
society.   We have just passed through the greatest
war in history which has quickened in men the habit
of questioning and seeking after something better.
Ours is the opportunity of applying on a greater scale
a conception and a method wherein lies a great hope.   It
is possible for any man to extend his circle of living
to meet laboring men and by offering himself as a
friend learn to understand the laboring man's point of
view, his despairs and his aspirations.

CHAPTER IV

FIRST CONTACT WITH THE SETTLEMENT

1. Not very long ago a stranger visiting New York City wanted to see the high buildings. The inspiration came to me to take him across the Brooklyn Bridge at about dusk so that as we walked back towards Manhattan the lights were coming on in the thousands of windows. As we neared the middle of the bridge we paused to watch the marvelous effect of the night enveloping the gleaming fairylike structures. Suddenly the stranger, turning his glance, noticed that there was complete darkness to the north of the bridge. "That's the East Side," I said, in explanation. But he wanted to know why it was not like the rest of the city. I explained that there were more people living there huddled together to the square foot than in any city in the world and that most of the houses did not have electricity. "What a contrast," he said as he looked back at the flashing buildings, "I never realized it was so near before."

2. The next day the stranger wanted to learn more, so we left the City Hall and walked out Madison Street, up Pitt Street, and then Avenue A to Fourteenth Street. It was a fairly comprehensive tour of those great neighborhoods commonly designated as the "Lower East Side." We made detours into Canal,

Rivington, Delancey, and Grand Streets, all important and busy thoroughfares, and the stranger learned one thing at least, that the East Side was not asleep. Business and industry cluttered up the streets, the sidewalks, the doorways, the halls and even the bedrooms of the over-crowded tenements. Everyone was trading or bargaining or hurrying somewhere with something. The children dodged pushcarts and trucks with equal ease. A pungent vegetable smell pervaded the air. The signs carried inscriptions in strange languages. There were dark doorways and long dark halls with a vista at the end of a drab back yard and perhaps an antiquated rear tenement beyond. In many cases the rooms inside were reached by long flights of wooden stairs, then more long dark hallways illuminated sometimes by a faint ray of daylight from a four foot court.

The stranger, who is unfamiliar with tenement conditions, is invariably impressed with the drab appearance of such a neighborhood, the eternal sameness and the eternal hopelessness of it all.

3. The average settlement is fairly conspicuous in such an atmosphere. Sandwiched in between tenement houses, perhaps actually occupying one of the old buildings, it will nevertheless wear a more cheerful aspect. A few judiciously placed flower boxes will advertise its presence. There may be a chattering group on the sidewalk. In the foyer there will be another group talking and seemingly not very much concerned about anything likely to happen.

4. It is a difficult task to adequately describe the impressions of one's first visit to a settlement. To

begin with, it makes a difference who you are. One is likely to forget that we always look at things through colored glasses as it were. The glasses represent our past experience, our natural background. When we look upon new things, we instinctively relate them to things that we already know. We compare things, we judge by standards. This accounts for the widely different first impressions that one gets of the settlement.

5. It sometimes happens that an apparently normal minded man will ask a conventionally minded friend to visit a settlement with him. It may be that the guest will go with some uncertainty as to whether there is to be revealed to him a sentimental weakness or possibly a religious fanaticism, heretofore unsuspected in his friend. A favorite method of introduction is to get the srtanger to take dinner with the residents. It will be a varied company. The women will probably be in the majority. There will be young women and middle aged; there will be the well dressed attractive type and beside her the so-called "New England schoolmarm." There will be long haired men in soft collars, whom the uninitiated will instantly suspect of socialism, as well as short haired men in business suits with conventional neck gear. There will be the inevitable buzz of conversation. Almost everyone will openly avow a genuine interest in what everyone else is doing and real importance will be attached to discussion of general topics of the day. There will be talking across the table, questionings, banterings, hasty opinions snapped and well considered opinions weighed. It is very possible that the visitor may feel himself

talked to, cornered, even patronized by some one whom he does not know, asked to come again and almost forced to accept an invitation for the following week.

I recite here the first impression of an actual settlement household. Sometimes one's experience is the opposite. I have sat at residents' tables and dragged through a meal making conversation about some trivial subject and without receiving the impression that the residents had one single atom of life or intelligence in their make up. The residents' table is very often the key to the spirit of the house.

6. The first impression of a settlement, however, is not always received through contact with the workers. Sometimes one will enter a settlement for the first time during the course of an evening when everything is running full blast. The bewildered visitor will be taken around and shown things. Most evident will be a gymnasium, filled with noisy athletes. It may be that the room will be given over to a dance and be filled with a crowd of happy and prosperous looking young people. It has been my privilege to give a great many people their first sight of a settlement and the comments elicited by the sight of the laughing crowd in the gymnasium have been most interesting. One man told me after coming several evenings, that he did not think he could give any more of his time. He said he felt that he could have given his time to relieve actual suffering but that the people who came to the settlement were all pretty well off anyway. His had evidently been only a superficial acquaintance, he had seen neither into the homes nor the hearts of those with whom he had come in contact. On the

other hand, I remember the experience of an emotional and sympathetic lady who had shown rare ability in assisting at the dances, dramatics, and other "evening affairs." Her usual method for getting to the settlement had been in the security of her motor, when the dinginess of the neighborhood had been cloaked in darkness. She came one morning in a clanging trolley through pushcart crowded street with the squalor of the garbage strewn courts bearing down upon her, and the pathos of the children sitting along the gutters playing upon her emotions. By the time she reached the settlement she was not the same woman that had presided so light-heartedly at the masques and dances.

One of the greatest sources of mystery to the casual visitor is the average settlement club. He has great difficulty in understanding its purposes. He insists generally upon calling it "a class." He assigns peculiar and limited reasons for its existence. I remember the case of a gentleman, who had been asked to be guest of honor at a club meeting, whose evident assumption was that the purpose of the club was to teach parliamentary procedure for he made the boys a speech, the burden of which was that he hoped that each and every one of them would realize his ambition and end up in Congress. Another visitor was shocked to learn that at some of the open forums at the settlement such subjects as socialism were discussed. One interested student sent for a visit to the settlement by his college Y. M. C. A., believing New York's lower east side to be an iniquitous resort, returned after seeing several "east side dance halls," to report to his fellow students: "Boys, it isn't like what you'd think! The dance halls weren't immoral at all!"

7. It is difficult to understand the settlement idea until one has carefully analyzed it. It has many sides and what is often the most evident is not of necessity the most important function. As Canon Barnett said, writing fourteen years after his first report, "Toynbee Hall seems to its visitors to be a center of education, a mission, a center of social effort. It may be so, but the visitors miss the truth that the place is a club house in Whitechapel occupied by men who do citizens' duty in the neighborhood. The residents are not as a body concerned for education, teetotalism, poor relief, or any special or sectarian object." It is often difficult for the outsider to discover what is the real underlying source of concern to the settlement worker. The reasons for the difficulty are the complexity of the activities themselves as well as the fact that what is often the most apparent to an observer is not necessarily the most fundamental or important work that is being carried on.

8. Of course it is evident at the outset that the people of the neighborhood who go to the settlement must have very different needs and purposes than have the residents who live there or even the volunteers whose activity is limited to regular visits to the house. Both the residents and the volunteers are representative of a class of people who have enjoyed peculiar advantages of education and position in society, while in general the people of the neighborhood represent those whose opportunities in life have been far more limited.

9. The obvious conclusion is that the first purpose of the settlement is to give to the people of the neighborhood some of the advantages which unfortunately have been denied to them. In a sense this is true, but in a sense only. The most immediate work that the settlement does is to give help where it is wanted but to give that help in a constructive way, so that, besides assisting immediately the individual in question, progress is at the same time made toward removing the social need for giving that particular kind of help to other individuals. To cite an example: a certain settlement in New York was called upon for assistance for distress arising out of gross negligence in a maternity case. Investigation revealed that a number of incompetent, dirty, and ignorant people were practicing midwifery in the neighborhood. Further research disclosed the fact that there was practically no control over the practice. As a result of this study all midwives in the city of New York must now be properly licensed before being permitted to practice.

10. In all of the work that the settlement is compelled to do it is not always so easy to distinguish the constructive social results that are sought after. A great deal of necessary work by its very nature can effect only those few who come directly into contact with the settlement and its staff of workers. When within the compass of a single tenement block many thousands live, who suffer continually for want of proper education and frequently for want of proper clothing, food and shelter, it is not encouraging to realize that the settlement at best may reach perhaps a hundred among the thousands. What the settlement

is able to do, in answer to the diversity of demands that are made upon it, seems pitifully little when the actual need is considered.   It is well to emphasize at this juncture to those who are discouraged, when they realize the small part that the settlement plays in giving immediate relief, that, as Canon Barnett said, it is not in this quarter that we are to look for the ultimate service that the settlement can render to society.

11.   The workings of the average settlement defy tabulation and analysis.   Not only is it perfectly impossible for any one man to know of all of the things which are being done by even the settlement in which he is living and working but in no two settlements is the method or the emphasis the same and in no one of them does it remain constant.   To be alive the settlement must continually be taking up new problems and seeking new ways with which to approach the older and more baffling questions.   I realize that no analysis that I can make can come within a measurable distance of covering the field.   It is nevertheless necessary to attempt some sort of classification.

12.   The settlement has a first hand contact first with its neighbors as individuals, secondly with the families of the neighborhood and thirdly with the neighborhood itself.   It has also a direct relation to the city and to the state.   It is in short an agency for interpreting society to itself in terms of the individuals and of the groups of individuals that go to make up the social body.   It has to deal both with the individual as a unit within the group and as an absolute individual. A large part of its task is to educate the individual to an understanding of his social relation to the group.

In addition there is the equally important task of educating the large group to an understanding and appreciation of the needs and limitations of the smaller component groups and of the individual. For the present we will limit ourselves to the discussion of the most immediate contacts of the settlement, namely with individuals and with the family.

13. The individuals who come to the settlement are of all ages and both sexes. The age divisions represent very young children, juniors, intermediates and seniors. There are fewer older people than there are numbers in any one of the divisions of young people. Within the age divisions there are classifications representing the different needs, capacities and tastes of the individuals. Among the younger people the club is the most usual unit which at once classifies the requirements of its members and furnishes the means of contact between the individual and the settlement.

14. The club system is an outgrowth of a natural development. By the time the average boy is eleven or twelve years old he tends to run with a gang. The gang is naturally invited into the settlement and as a result the club is evolved. As a rule both girls' and boys' departments are organized under the club system. With the older people this spirit is not so strong. The point of contact is more likely to be because of interest in the family or through general sympathy with the activities of the house. Before we are in a position to discuss club work in detail or to enter into any comprehensive study of the various other intricate influences and activities of the settlement, we must come

to an understanding of certain principles and must arrive at some sort of definite answer to several fundamental questions.

15. What do the many individualities with their varying tastes who come to the settlement seek? What are their needs? Is there something among their multitude of desires that they crave in common? First and foremost they seek *recreation*; and by that I mean re-creation in the broadest sense of the word. Scarcely less eagerly, though perhaps not with the same degree of self consciousness, they seek *education*. I believe that the great mass of men, women and young people, considered as individuals, are seeking to satisfy one or both of these ends, when they turn to settlements, and I mean here to include church houses and allied associations such as the Y. M. C. A. and Y. M. H. A.

16. When the family comes to the settlement the case is somewhat different. Generally aid is sought because of acute distress where neither the individual nor the united efforts of the family are capable of bringing relief. The two major difficulties are *health* and *financial distress*. Another frequent cause of trouble involving the family is *conduct*.

17. The immediate articulate demands that are made on the settlement by individuals or by families may be summarized therefore by these five captions: *recreation, education, health, financial distress,* and *conduct*. Because I have assigned the first two to needs that are most likely to be expressed through individuals, I do not mean to imply that the demand is restricted in that sense, nor do I mean to imply that the last three types of calls come only through the

family. I have made this classification, because it expresses the most usual course of things. It must not be supposed for one instant, that the demands, which I have set down above are special demands made only upon the settlement. They are the natural demands which have always become vocal whenever human life is cramped and deprived of proper outlet. In a certain measure there have always been those who have striven to keep human life fresh and wholesome and where there has been recognition of a need, there has been an attempt to fill it. The way that this has been done has been dependent upon the viewpoint of those who have attempted to answer the demand.

18. The founding of "home missions" for instance was an original attempt on the part of those who felt that the greatest human need was to stamp out wickedness. The movement was inspired by a desire to "rescue" the poor man from degradation and to protect him from evil. It might be said that the attitude of mind of the directing forces was controlled by the wickedness point of view. Now in all movements for social betterment the point of view of the forces directing the movement is of the utmost importance. There exist movements whose point of view is strictly sectarian and whose chief effort is to gain adherents who can be made to subscribe to the rules of the particular sect. It cannot be denied that such adherence to a set of rules is undoubtedly a valuable influence in regulating conduct. Then there is the distress relief viewpoint. Nineteenth Century "charity" was largely concerned with giving outright for the relief of the poor in distress. There will probably

always exist the need for immediate relief in cases of emergency but it is now generally recognized that the giving of such relief does absolutely nothing toward relieving the causes of such distress. So also of the health viewpoint. There is today no social need more widely recognized than that of caring for those suffering from sickness or disease. Our well organzied hospital system attests the truth of this. But it is known that mal-nutrition, bad air, and bad housing conditions are the direct causes of most sickness and disease. It is recognized that unsatisfactory industrial conditions have played a dominating and many times a merciless part in the undoing of the workman and the laborer. At times industry has not seemed able to support the population in health and happiness. Looking at the social problem from this angle, one can understand the strictly economic point of view which interprets economics in terms of unyielding law.

19. It was the growth of the friendly or humanitarian view point which first inspired the form of living which has developed into the settlement idea. The spirit of humility and open mindedness, which dominated this latter movement, made it possible to attempt to analyze economic theory, and to add to it a realization that the social desires of man may be organized to control economic law. It might be said that the resultant has been the development of the modern socio-economic viewpoint which takes into consideration social organization and the relation thereto of human needs and motives. At the present writing this is the broadest conceivable ground for an approach to the problem of the improvement of human society.

While taking the broad ground, the settlement recognizes the value of the many other viewpoints that may be taken. It must be concerned in the many differing programs that are put forward. It must take an active part in many of them but it must not make any one of them its primary concern. The central philosophy of the socio-economic view point must be allowed to dominate. This will mean the weighing of all programs for their social value. It involves inquiry into the agencies existing within the organization of society for the satisfaction of human wants as well as inquiry into the faults of organization which either retard or prevent satisfaction of these wants. In any attempt at social improvement the value of the viewpoint of the forces directing the improvement cannot be over-emphasized.

20. I have therefore attempted to recapitulate the various types of viewpoint which exercise social control.

The wickedness viewpoint.
The sectarian viewpoint.
The distress relief viewpoint.
The educational viewpoint.
The recreational viewpoint.
The friendly or humanitarian viewpoint.
The health viewpoint.
The industrial viewpoint.
The economic viewpoint.
The psychological viewpoint.
The socio-economic viewpoint.

If the last named viewpoint may be said to be the

dominant factor in social work today, it must be understood that the other viewpoints are clearly recognized as factors bearing a functional relation to the central socio-economic philosophy. In the next chapter it will be our purpose to inquire into methods of settlement work and we shall find the activities organized along functional lines which are analagous to these view points and which have as their object the fulfillment of the five types of demands which the individual and the family are likely to make upon the settlement.

CHAPTER V

1. When a single organization is called upon to stand for and give effective assistance in widely differing directions, it must indeed be an organization. It cannot haphazard at one time help those who crave intellectual culture, those who seek both mental and physical relaxation, and those who suffer for lack of proper clothing, food, and shelter.

The usual form, which the organization of the average settlement takes, is the subdivision of the activities into clubs, classes, gymnasium work, dances, dramatics, concerts, illustrated lectures, debating societies, game rooms, health work, musical work, art work, case work, neighborhood work, and general events of a social nature. It is not difficult to see that these activities are intended to represent the settlement's answer to the demands which are made upon it by the neighborhood. To the outsider and to the uninitiated, however, the complexity of the miscellaneous forms of work is a source of confusion. When one sees a great many things being done at the same time, it is not easy to arrive at a correct understanding of their interrelation and of the fundamental purpose governing all of them.

To me it is helpful to think of the settlement as

attempting two classes of work: Regular work and Extension work.

2.   Regular work consists of those activities which, it has been found practical to standardize. The great bulk of recreational and educational work is a ready subject for standardization. Where it is necessary to depend upon a constantly changing set of workers, the setting of the standard is a safeguard against the unnecessary waste and deterioration of hit and miss methods. One might say that the mere maintenance of the settlement house at a given level of efficiency is regular work. To keep the building itself clean and fresh, to provide meeting places and proper leadership for the number of clubs connected with the settlement, to keep up the purely educational work of the house involves the maintenance of a standard. Indeed, it is possible to run what is sometimes called a successful recreational and educational center without introducing one new idea after the original standard has been set, or without the workers being compelled to step outside the door of their settlement.

3.   No amount of standardization, no matter how well it may be carried out, can do away with the necessity for effective extension work. Where the settlement becomes a self-contained and self-sufficient institution, it begins to lose vitality and it is certain to get out of touch with its neighborhood. Work among the younger people may still continue unchallenged but the older element will begin falling away. When this happens it is generally a certain sign that the settlement is becoming ingrowing.

It is difficult to make clear just what is meant by

the term "extension work." It should not be confused with the term "extension teaching" as used by our universities and schools to denote extending the benefits of the university to pupils not connected with it as matriculates. I do not intend any such limited meaning. When I speak of "extension work," I mean original work on the part of the settlement, along untried lines. When a group of fifteen to twenty boys of approximately the same age are organized into a club and brought into the settlement under a director, it is merely part of the regular work of the house. If, however, a special type of club, consisting of say, eight or ten boys, were organized to meet weekly, by turns, at one of the boy's homes and monthly at the settlement, such an enterprise would today be extension work. Again, if to meet a particular situation, such as the housing shortage, a tenants' association is formed with the assistance of the settlement, it is extension work. If, on the other hand, a single resident or worker at the settlement pays a friendly call in the neighborhood, it is one of the simplest types of extension work. If, for any particular need, a definite survey is organized by the settlement, it is another type of the same work.

The full significance of extension work will be better understood after we have come to an understanding of the more permanent benefits of the settlement method. It is necessary at this point only to stress the fact that no real social progress is possible unless great care and thought are continually put into the extension work. It is essential that due emphasis be placed upon this before we enter into a detailed discussion of the more regular activities.

4. Among all the facilities offered by the settlement, those for recreation are the most readily made use of. There are those who claim that altogether too much time and space are given over to recreation. He would be a prophet indeed who could draw the line. When we recall the incident of the busy man who withdrew from settlement work because everybody was having such a good time that he felt he wasn't needed, we are forced to admit that there was justice in his criticism. He had evidently come in contact with well standardized regular work. He had not understood the problem as a whole.

5. Recreation is one of the fundamental needs of all human beings. There are a cultivated few whose recreation takes the higher form of inspirational devotion to one of the arts. Strangely enough the dividing line is not drawn here between rich and poor and between those who have had the advantages of education and those who have not. There are as many among the unlearned poor who crave recreation of a higher sort as there are those among the educated well-to-do who are bored with what they dub "highbrow stuff." No doubt but that the settlement can minister here to a very real want. The understanding that some forms of education may be an intellectual recreation to starved minds should answer those critics who contend that public educational effort should be "practical" and should not aim to reach cultural levels.

For the great mass of human beings no doubt, recreation means principally relaxation. The need is vital.

Industrial and clerical workers must have relaxation. It is a need which society must provide. That society does not provide satisfactory or ample opportunities has been recognized by many of our great industrial concerns, who have gone in some cases to extreme lengths to provide recreational facilities for their employes. There was hardly a manufacturing concern in the United States of importance in the Great War that did not have some kind of an organization for getting its employes together and giving them decent recreational facilities. In many cases the Government, in addition to its housing program, undertook to provide some means of recreation. There is not space to recount here the remarkable progress that was made both by the Government and industrial companies during the war. It is significant, however, that manufacturing plants are uniformly anxious to keep up this sort of work. "It pays!" But there are countless workers who are not benefited by the facilities offered by large business. Little has yet been done for employes in the municipal, state, and federal civil services. Then there are always the backward industries and the backward employers. The demands of an industrial and commercial community for recreation appear insatiable and the settlement, in the recreational field alone will be taxed to greater limits than it can provide for. The settlement must minister to this vital human need. The relaxation must be provided. This will be the most evident, though not necessarily the most important, part of its activities.

6. When the tired worker has re-created himself he will be the better citizen. The settlement must

be ready with a more direct appeal to those who are grateful and happy for the recreational facilities and simple human intercourse they have enjoyed. It is just at this point that many social settlements break down. It often seems as though the average house had nothing further to offer. Where this is true the settlement is little more useful than the average movie house or dance hall and certainly not as desirable though perhaps more popular than any church house or even one of the small Y. M. C. A.'s.

7. Intelligent extension work has been one of the forces that has kept the settlement movement vital. Many of the special investigations have revealed neglected phases of life and have helped to liberate valuable social forces. Frequently the need has been sufficient to warrant the development of a new line of activity at the settlement even to the point of standardization. Take for example the attempt of settlements to satisfy the demands made upon them for music and for instruction in music. The pioneer in this direction was the Music School Settlement in New York. It was organized with the avowed purpose of putting a special work to the test. It was marvelously successful. Other settlements in the city were called upon to give better opportunities for musical work. They began to develop "music departments." Today regular music schools exist in the majority of the more important houses, and these are joined together in a Federation of Music Schools.

8. Another demand, which has been made upon the settlements, is that they supply some outlet for those who would express themselves by the graphic

arts. The desire to draw, to model, or to create is an indication of the artist's impulse to express life and truth as he understands it. As Robert Browning put it:

" . . . we're made so that we love
First when we see them painted, things we have
    passed
Perhaps a hundred times nor cared to see;
. . .
God uses us to help each other so,
Lending our minds out."

In settlement neighborhoods, even among those people who have had few educational advantages, there are minds who see life clearly. The settlement can assist not only by supplying the natural cultural background, which is necessary, but by directing and teaching the technique of expression in the particular arts. Greenwich house in New York City was one of the pioneers in this. Remarkable work has been done in developing the artistic impulses among immigrant nationalities. Most settlements have made some sort of similar effort but the development has not been carried as far as it has with music. A possible explanation is the fact that free education in art has already become more firmly established through other agencies. Public schools and colleges give courses in art. I do not mean to say that art education in America is what it should be, but it has at least become established. It is the settlement's present task to supplement, to advise, and to encourage.

9. In connection with dramatics, a great deal has been accomplished. Beginning with amateur theatricals the work has widened out until it has realized more

far reaching possibilities. The Hull House Players in Chicago have won a notable name for themselves. In Henry Street, in New York, dramatics have drawn a clientele that a few years ago warranted the establishment of the Neighborhood Theater on Grand Street. Here it has been possible to attempt to relate literature, the drama, and the graphic arts. The theater possesses very complete equipment in the way of work shops for the making of its own scenery, equipment and costumes.

It is only recently that the power of the drama as a living force in daily life has been appreciated. Not only is it an educational force along intellectual and spiritual lines, but it offers first hand to the individual, a vision of the possibilities of self development and self equipment for the positive business of everyday existence. To get the force of this, one has to witness the awakening of a drab personality, stirred by the imaginative possibilities and the mock realities of the stage. Through pronouncing words of genius, which are put into one's mouth, one learns the attributes of genius and begins, unconsciously at first, to equip oneself for a fuller and more purposeful part in society. It is of great educational value to witness the acting of a good play, but to walk upon the stage, to speak to hushed audiences is to awake to a consciousness of power generally unsuspected within the self. When the settlement sponsors the drama, it should be with this view. Because the dramatic form is used, it does not mean that the settlement through it is trying to create professional actors, any more than, because parliamentary procedure is used in the clubs, it means that the settlement is trying to create professional representatives and senators.

10.   The encouragement of debates and public speaking is with a similar purpose.   It is of the greatest value for creating self confidence with the individual and for giving him the simplest means of self expression.   Almost every settlement makes some attempt at holding open forums and encouraging the discussion of social questions.   The open forum is a great agency for awakening people to a sense of their community of interest and for furnishing a direct agency both for the expression and execution of community desires. Once the settlement has made its place and won the trust of those who live crowded up to its doors, there is no limit to its usefulness.   Intelligent organization and assistance are all that are needed to bring out local opinion.   Where the settlement is alive to the possibilities of extension work, it will find that it is constantly called upon by the neighborhood.   Confidence in the settlement is easily bred by fearless support of neighborhood needs, and confidence makes opinion vocal. Many of the civic improvements, which have been made in recent years, have been matured from small beginnings and brought to expression through the settlements.   The University Settlement wielded great influence in the Delancey Street improvement in New York at the time of the opening of the Williamsburgh Bridge.   The neighborhood wanted it.   The settlement helped to give expression to this sentiment.   Indeed, when neighborhoods speak through settlements the voice is very nearly an imperative.

11.   In addition to local questions, the settlement

serves as an agency for crystalizing opinion in regard
to public policy. During the past decade and a half
there has been a great deal of what has been termed
remedial legislation. Latterly, perhaps in realization
that it was the social rather than the political structure
that was ailing, this movement has been termed social
legislation. The forces of organized labor have been
responsible for much of the pressure that has been
brought to bear upon our legislators but many of the
cold hard facts, certainly the best surveys and probably
the most adequate knowledge has been supplied by
workers in our settlements. There is no more valuable
work that is done by the settlements than this of
supplying accurate knowledge of living conditions in
tenement neighborhoods. Where social legislation is
necessary we are turning more and more to social
workers for advice. It is impossible to conceive of
any more first hand method of getting information
to direct public action, than to turn to those leaders,
who, while sharing the life of people whose horizon is
beset with obstacles, are using their own trained intelligence to make better living conditions possible. It is
to be regretted that much of the information, which
is gathered together, is completely lost to the public
because it is not put into proper form to make it available. *The "Survey"* has given valuable assistance here
through publishing the results of investigations in its
columns. Settlements should make a greater use of
this valuable publicity agency.

12. There has recently developed in New York
and other cities as an outgrowth of the settlement,
another activity of which a word must be said in

passing. It is the recreation and social center activity organized in the public schools. This development represents the enlarging of the settlement idea. The essential difference is that there is no one in residence. It is the people's social center with the emphasis on the recreation and the town meeting or open forum. Similar centers of public recreation are the municipal baths and gymnasiums and the town free libraries. Many municipalities are even going so far as to attempt to furnish "play directors" for the children in some of the public gardens.

13. During the war there developed in the United States a movement which promises very far reaching results unless it is prostituted by individuals seeking personal preferment. The movement reached its maturest state in Cincinnati, Ohio, where the Social Unit plan was developed. In the fall of 1919 a definite attempt was made to turn the so-called Community Councils of National Defense into permanent Community Councils organized for the purpose of advancing neighborhood welfare.

The movement bears a resemblance to the old Neighborhood Associations which were an outgrowth of settlement work and which did go a great way toward getting local opinion together. The Community Council, however, appears to be more general in its make-up, all individuals in the neighborhood being invited to take part in its meetings. The Councils seem to have sprung up in many cases outside of already organized agencies of opinion. In every case they certainly have the virtue of stimulating local thought. It is a plan which social settlements and social organizations in general have wished well for but there are many difficulties to be overcome and much educational work to be done. In such work the settlements undoubtedly will take an important part.

14. I have given as one of the principal demands, to which the settlement must respond the caption "financial distress." More often than the individual it is the family that feels this distress acutely. When the family finds itself in dire straits the relief to be effective must be immediate. Though the settlement receives many such calls and must be prepared to act immediately, it is not the only agency that receives them. The church has always been guardian angel of the needy poor.

15. Within the last twenty years there has grown up another agency, represented by so-called "Organized Charity." This is composed in New York City of the Charity Organization Society, the Association for Improving the Condition of the Poor, and the United Hebrew Charities. Other cities support similar organizations. These great impersonal organized charities have their supporters who pay out their money and have the assurance that it is scientifically distributed. Undoubtedly a very necessary piece of work is done but the scientific administration is of course expensive. Acting as a clearing house for the great organized charities there is generally an organization such as the Social Service Exchange in New York. The mere keeping of reliable central records is a protection to the community against "being worked for charity." Reference to this clearing center is necessary if efficient neighborhood case work is to be done by the settlement.

It is to be hoped that the impersonality of the great "organized" societies can be made up for by closer co-operation with the human touch of the social settlement and the lackadaisical method of working and keeping records, often a fault in the settlement, may be improved by contact with the system of the societies.

16. By virtue of their character, the societies can only give the most immediate relief. It is an expense to "carry a case." As a result we have what are termed "closed cases," which means, in brief, that the relief proscribed has been administered and that the society has turned to other work. Settlements through the means of friendly visiting, are able to keep in touch with families, who have been helped and often are able to prevent recurrences of distress by timely assistance or advice before the trouble again becomes acute. With the settlement there should be no such thing as a closed case.

17. Case work is, however, in reality mere emergency work. It must not be made an end in itself. There must always be the vision in the settlement looking toward removing the causes of distress. The problems that arise when such an attitude is taken will be discussed in their place. It is merely desired to comment here on the hard fact that in the constantly arising emergencies, the settlement is called on to act for immediate results. Hunger and disease do not await social readjustment to reap their victims, whom poverty and filth and ignorance have prepared for them. The settlement must minister to the hungry and sick. It must act as adviser and friend to needy individuals and families, helping them out of difficulties

and tiding them over critical times, often giving employment, sometimes making possible fresh air vacations. Sometimes as in the winter of 1913-1914, the settlement is called upon to face the actual difficulties of general unemployment. The report of the University Settlement of N. Y. for 1913 illustrates the lengths to which it may be necessary to go to relieve acute distress. It reads:

"As this report goes to press an emergency, due to a combination of causes, has arisen which the settlement is trying to meet. The intense cold weather and the large number of unemployed men, have made it seem wise to give each night shelter to as many men as the floor space of our Assembly and Guild Halls can accommodate, . . . providing a simple breakfast of coffee and rolls at a nearby restaurant."

Here is an activity which is nothing more than a makeshift. It was done because it had to be done and the settlement was on the ground and understood the conditions. The immediacy of the distress was great enough to cause the settlement to attack the problem from an angle entirely different from its regular course, which would have been to hunt jobs for the men and look into the causes of their unemployment.

18. The settlement has gone far to meet the causes of distress due to health which are likely to be brought to its door. In fact one house, the Henry Street Settlement,[*] has developed a visiting nurse service, which may be weighed favorably against all the other direct benefits of settlement work for the good that has

---

[*] See "The House on Henry Street," by Lillian D. Wald. See also Reports.

been accomplished. New York City has been districted and from the various centers nurses are sent out upon reports of need coming in through physicians, insurance companies, charities, families, or other sources. In the year 1920 the staff averaged 212 members, 336,722 visits were made to 42,902 patients. The work is supported by gifts, endowment, and payments from the insurance companies, and from those receiving treatment. The work has gone far indeed but it is capable of still further development. Municipalities, counties, and communities have taken up the idea. The district nurse is known all over the United States.

19. Almost all settlements will make the attempt to have at least one resident with a nurse's training and to work through her in connection with the regular district nursing service. The resident nurse should have the health work of the settlement under her care. She should be responsible for the health education of the neighborhood. She should relate the settlement to the organized work of maternity centers, milk stations, diet kitchens, free clinics, and other health agencies. If the neighborhood is one where these are undeveloped, there will be all the more call for the resident nurse in the settlement, for it will be necessary to start out upon a constructive campaign to gain for the district the health agencies which it lacks. Such a campaign will require trained leadership. The resident nurse will always have a wide field in health extension work, in the detection and care of mental defectives, as well as the study of particular classes of health cases. At one time Union Settlement in

New York supported a school for anaemic children on its roof. The settlement is strategically placed for dealing intelligently with some of the most perplexing health problems which are confronting society.

20. There is no doubt but that there are many social agencies long in existence as well as those forces which have been set in motion by the war which are only beginning to realize the entrée which the social settlement can give them into the very fields of endeavor which they seek. There is little doubt but that the Day Nursery, palliative though it may be, operates with greater usefulness when balanced by the social service work of a nearby settlement. There is little doubt but that the settlement must call again and again upon the Day Nursery for vital assistance in its neighborhood.

21. Another call which is regularly made upon the settlement organization is to help the individual and the family in cases arising from conduct. The simple friendships between the residents and their neighbors are of the greatest value here; for after all, friendship is one of the most helpful of human relationships. Where conduct goes far in the wrong direction it is sure to come sharply against the rigidity of the civil and the criminal law. The law, however, is not very generally understood by the uneducated man and the foreigner. Indeed its perplexities continually baffle the understanding of many of the most intelligent. A man of means can retain a lawyer to advise him. The poor man is often the victim of the shyster. Settlements either directly or in co-operation with Legal Aid Societies should be equipped when called upon

to make the law intelligible to the poor man and to assure him that he gets a square deal.

22. In this connection, settlements are continually called upon to co-operate with other organizations. Valuable assistance has been rendered to the Courts in making their probation work effective, and there has been mutual co-operation with the work of such organizations as the "Big Brothers," the "Big Sisters," and "Juvenile Protective Societies." [7] There is much to be gained on both sides by such co-operation. The settlement has its entrée into the neighborhood and its wide viewpoint to balance against a particular program and a special understanding. It is to be hoped that, as time goes on, organized social forces will become more and more closely knit and that co-operation will become more and more extensive as understanding increases.

---

[7] Especially see Bibliography for reports by Juvenile Protective Association of Chicago.

CHAPTER VI

1. In meeting the recreational and educational demands that are made upon it, the policy of the average settlement is so bound up with the administration of its club system that it is well to inquire further into the latter before attempting to study the deeper social significance of the movement as a whole. As has been already pointed out, the club is the most typical unit of individuals with which the settlement deals. It differs from the class, which it often appears to resemble, by having a more closely knit existence. The members are bound together by particular ties such as friendship or a common interest in the purposes of the club. Generally a written constitution is the basis of organization. The membership is elective. By its members the club form is at first used to give expression and stability to the requirements of everyday social intercourse. It soon becomes a regular source of recreational enjoyment and in time its educational potentialities are realized.

2. Long experience has given to the settlement an understanding of the possibilities to be realized in club work as well as knowledge of the difficulties to be encountered so that the average house has, ready to be put into operation, what might be termed a regular

club program. When the settlement furnishes meeting rooms for the club and either invites or permits the latter to join its organization, it assumes a responsibility. For this reason a representative of the settlement, usually an older and more experienced person, generally meets with the club in the capacity of director. It is his business to see that the club gets the benefit of the advantages which the settlement is able to offer.

3. The position of club director is exceedingly delicate and is one which calls for great tact and forebearance. Club work to be effective should be a natural expression of the members themselves. The director must exercise a nice balance. He can lead but he cannot push. He can point to errors, he can warn of mistakes. He should not, however, insist upon definite or specific action. The ideal director is hard to find. The average beginner is so little appreciative of the necessity for regularity that he is apt to be undependable. It is very frequently the fault of the settlement that he isn't started right. He is often given charge of a club before he understands the nature of the task before him. Many times he is allowed to founder without support and without receiving an inkling of the existence of the great mass of settlement experience with clubs, amid which he is working. Where he is properly supported and where he has imagination to grasp the possibilities the untried volunteer can bring a certain freshness into club leadership which is often missing in the work of the professional.

4. One of the hardest tasks, which the settlement has, is to find a sufficient number of the right kind

of club leaders. The house staff is not large enough to be depended upon. Indeed their energies will be freer for general work in the settlement if, so far as clubs are concerned, their activities are limited to general supervision and guidance. The actual leadership of the individual clubs may be handed over entirely to volunteers. This means that the responsibility for securing these volunteers must be placed upon capable shoulders. It is a very general fault, however, that this responsibility is never very definitely located. I know of one or two settlements that have volunteer committees charged with the task of "getting new friends interested" to give their personal service. The difficulties in the way are realized and the failures are easily excused. The problem is attacked piecemeal from the point of view of getting a leader for one little club or for one little settlement. The one leader may be procured but, for the same amount of effort something much more far reaching ought to be accomplished.

The problem should be appreciated and approached in its full magnitude. It is the problem of securing volunteers for social work. Settlement work and social work ought to be carried on ninety per cent by volunteers. The professional worker is a necessary evil. He plays a vital part but it is only a part. The settlement idea is a method of living and unless the method becomes far better understood and more generally practiced than it has up to now, it will perish and all its promise will be dissipated. Volunteers will not be found for the settlement in any such numbers as they are needed, until all social agencies unite in a campaign to popularize the settlement idea and so make it comprehensible to the man in the street as a method of life quite within the range of practicability.

A slight beginning has been made in the way of an attempt "to get the colleges interested." Students have been approached, and have been urged "to go into social work," much in the same way as they have been urged to go into scientific work, banking, or what not. It has not been made sufficiently apparent, however, that they can play a part in social work at the same time that they are pursuing their regular business or vocation. Discussion of how the settlement movement is to carry on may properly be left to the concluding chapter, it is necessary to comment here only upon the hard fact that, in order to carry on regular club work, there must be a constant supply of volunteer leaders ready and interested to give personal service. Incidentally I have heard many headworkers say, "We want busy men and women for our volunteers; it doesn't pay to ask people to help who have time on their hands."

5. The busy man or woman has a better sense of responsibility and is better equipped to win the respect of the club members than one who has no sense of the value of time nor of the necessity for holding to obligations. In club leadership it is the value of example that counts. The members of the club will do what they observe the person to do, whom they respect the most. If that person is the club director he will not have to tell them anything.

Let me cite an example. A certain group of boys averaging about fifteen or sixteen years got the reputation of being "the toughest bunch on the block." They used to stand around drug stores and side doors of saloons smoking very cheap cigarettes and cat-calling at the girls who passed by. They had a scorn for the conventional type of hats and affected big caps pulled over their ears at curious angles. They had a peculiar way of spitting out of the corners of their mouths. They punctuated their sentences with words like Jesus and damn and hell, and others not so nice in their original meaning. They spent their evenings provoking trouble and hunting for excitement. One night they visited the neighborhood dance in progress at a settlement (Admission 5 cents). Two of them were kicked out for refusing to take off their caps, another was evicted for a rough house that ended in breaking a chair, a fourth was put out for using profane language. Three remained. They were engaged in conversation by a very large man whom they later learned had been a famous football player at Princeton. They were interested in the gymnasium equipment. The idea came to them that basketball could be played by boys who didn't go to high school. They asked if they could play. They were told that if they formed a club and had a director that they could play. They asked the big man to be their director and said that they would get the rest of their "bunch." But the rest of the bunch resentful over having been put out, refused to come in. They asked the big man if he would come and talk to the others. He did. He spent an evening with them. Where they went he went also, but they noticed that he didn't cat-call after girls and that he didn't wear a cap.

6. They came to the settlement house again and asked him to spend another evening with them. The big man said he didn't much enjoy dancing on cellar doors and proposed that they should go to a show. Two of them hadn't any money and asked him to wait while they "swiped a nickel off the soda and candy man at the corner." He said he'd lend them the money. They said that would be all right that "they'd swipe it later." They noticed that he took off his hat when he went into the movie house. They asked if they couldn't form a club and play basketball. He helped them start their club. They found they couldn't go on the gymnasium floor without rubber soled shoes. They said they guessed the house wasn't for them but only for "swells." The big man suggested that they earn some money and buy the shoes. Three of them did. One swapped his regular shoes for tennis shoes. Another complained that he had to give all his money to his mother. The others laughed; the big man didn't. Next week he had a pair of shoes to lend.

7. Then they discovered that everyone else paid dues to their club and that the club paid five dollars a year to the house for the use of the gymnasium. There was a cry of protest but the big man said he'd trust them until they earned it. He said that he had had to borrow money himself to go through college and that he'd just finished paying it back. They remarked that he must have wanted to go awfully bad. He asked how many of them were going to high school. Nobody answered. Then one of the boys asked what's the use. The big man said that if he didn't know himself he guessed there wasn't any use. As time went on

the boys asked questions. Half of the time they received no direct reply. They learned to observe as well as to inquire. They began to have an understanding of the value of some of the things that they had laughed at. They left off sneering and cat-calling.

8. They were ordinary boys, typical of hundreds who are formed into clubs and of a type with stuff in them worth developing. It took simply contact with something a little better than street corner standards to win their devotion. It must not be assumed, however, that club work is something that runs easily and develops all by itself without a struggle. It is a succession of problems one after the other. Very young children require a different sort of handling from the club of boys of whom I have given an account. For a time the boys and girls work is better separated. Then, as the age of adolescence approaches, the problem is to get them together again in a natural way. Aside from the regular program of club work, club "affairs" are periodically arranged for. At these the members of the club giving the "affair" are the responsible hosts. The guests are members of other clubs or outsiders who have no connection with the house; they are both girls and boys. It is surprising how zealously standards are guarded at these affairs. Each club is desirous of making its affair the best and "the finest thing that has been done."

9. The great criticism of the club system is that it leads nowhere. The clubs are carried to a certain point of development only to disband, or to loose interest in the house, or perhaps to change character completely as the members grow maturer. The club pro-

gram seems apparently to have no end which it has been found possible to achieve. If by that is meant a definite and finite end then the answer is that it has none. When, however, one stops to consider the great number of individuals for whom the club has been the means to a larger understanding of life as well as a preparation for life, it is no mean achievement. The aim of club work should not be confused with the aim of settlement work. The spirit of the latter should dominate the former but individual clubs should not be expected to flower into small imitations of the millenium.

10. The organization which has grown up side by side with the settlement, of which the Boys' Club of New York on Avenue A is typical, exists solely for the purpose of work with boys. There is less reason for confusion as to its aims. This type of self-contained Boys' Club has amply justified its existence. There is no excuse for badly done club work. The study of the boy, his development, his needs, and his training is the first and foremost object of the leaders as well as of all of the workers in the movement. There is no chance that planning a program for the boys will be relegated to a secondary place. The broader scope and purpose of the settlement require that first thought be given to broad social considerations which often necessitate the assignment of the administration of the boys' and girls' departments to subordinates. This should not mean that the work is not just as well done. In practice, however, it means that leadership is more temporary and that the settlements are constantly resorting to makeshifts and com-

plaining that they never seem to be able to find just the right sort of man or woman to take over the responsibility of the boys' or the girls' department.

It is my belief that settlements have a great deal to learn from the more specialized work of the organized Boys' Clubs. This is particularly true of New York City, where, but for one or two exceptions, this sort of work is far behind what has been done in some of the lesser cities. There is in existence an International Federation of Boys Clubs, membership in which should be extremely helpful to the boys departments of the settlements. There is also a national organization of girls clubs. The possibilities for cooperative helpfulness in both of these movements are unbounded.

11.   Space does not permit a profound discussion of the interesting details of what has come to be known as boys' work and girls' work. It is impossible, however, to pass on without a mention of the organization known as the Boy Scouts of America. There is also a counterpart among the girls. At the present time, the movement seems to be somewhat top heavy. This is due probably to its semi-military form. It is built from the top down, each unit deriving its authority for existence from the unit immediately above. Quite a large paper organization is therefore required to support a single troop in the field. Undoubtedly the movement will grow to fit the framework. Occasionally, however, one is brought face to face with the feeling of healthy scorn with which some of those in the field regard their paper officials.

The most significant development that has taken

place recently has been the adoption by settlements of the Boy Scout program as their method in boys' work. Where this has been done, so far as has come to my knowledge, it has met with unqualified success. To city boys, the out of door part of the program has been of more than especial value; it has been a revelation. What may be ultimately accomplished appears to be limited only by the leadership that will be available. Notwithstanding their more definitely mapped program, it has been no easier to find scoutmasters than directors of boys' clubs. The Scout organization itself has so far disclaimed the responsibility for providing leaders. It has offered, however, to train any number of leaders in scouting as soon as they were provided by the settlements and other organizations standing sponsor for troops, and it has offered to exercise supervision over both leader and troop. Despite this willingness there has not been shown, especially by the minor officials of the movement, an appreciation of the fact that scouting is a specialized form of boys' work and as such merely a phase of social work. The scouts have not been conscious of their relationship to the social movement as a whole nor have they been awake either to the need or to the part they should play in a concerted and continuous campaign for volunteers for social work.

THE SUMMER CAMP

12. Before closing there is a certain branch of settlement work which has been very definitely organized that should properly be discussed in this chapter.

While it cannot be said that the summer camp is an integral part of the house proper it has certainly come to be regarded as a very necessary adjunct. Settlement work is hardly looked upon as complete unless it can offer fresh air relief in necessitous cases. Superficially there is no reason why the camp should be under the same administration as the city house; fundamentally and in practice, however, there are many advantages.

In the first place any program for recreation in the summer months is barren unless it includes an attempt to get out into the air and into the country. In the second place summer weather is too hot for carrying on much of the indoor club work which is the rule in winter. In the third place the children and younger people are out of school and thrown upon the streets in the hot weather. Finally it is much easier to raise money for fresh air vacations in the country than for perhaps any of the many other activities for which the settlement is sponsor. It is thus often possible to transport a portion of the house staff to camp and to carry on there certain of the regular activities under a modified form.

13. At the camp, however, the home, the family, and the neighborhood are all removed from the round of everyday life. Those who go to the camp are therefore taken outside of their natural environment. One may think of them as individualities literally turned loose. It is of very distinct value to each of them to experience this feeling of complete freedom, of the throwing off of chains as it were; but it will be balanced on the other hand by a closer association with

certain positive and established forces than prevailed in the settlement. Contact with the residents will be more continuous than was possible in the city. There is no doubt but that some of the most intensive work so far as girls and boys are concerned, is best accomplished at the summer camp.

As a rule the boys' work is conducted separately from the girls'. There are camps, however, where a complete community is the basis of organization. At Northover Camp, at Bound Brook, N. J., there is a division for girls, for boys, for younger girls, for younger boys, and also for older people, but there are many things that daily bring the whole community together. Classified work is possible but there is in addition the advantage of an inter-related social group. Young people are thrown naturally together without interference from some of the conventional barriers which so often are a source of misconception and misinterpretation. It becomes possible for those of the opposite sexes to meet on the basis of friendship outside of a dance hall without the imputation that they are "keeping company."

The big common dining room is a valuable social center. It is not for the purpose of keeping order that a resident is placed at each table, but to act as host, to keep things running smoothly, and to make those, who are not used to big dining rooms, feel at home. I remember distinctly the case of a city school teacher, who, after spending a two weeks' vacation at such a camp, went to the headworker to say, "Do you know? I'm a plain man, I've worked my own way, I've given myself my education. I've been able to get a great many things for myself, but there's something I'd like to tell you, I've never had the chance before to eat with ladies and gentlemen at the same table, and it's meant a great deal to me, though it's very hard for me to explain it to you."

14.   Camp life has an extraordinary value because it is an exceedingly democratic life.   It is possible for people, whose usual interests and experiences have been diametrically opposite, to find a common interest in the more primitive pleasures and duties of life in camp.   Out on a hike with the boys social differences are non-existent.   Life appears broader and more human.   Here is an inkling, a vision, of the possibilities that lie in the settlement idea.   To share life with others, to find joys, simple though they may be, that can be shared with an ever widening circle, is to discover that men have many things in common.   After all, it is shared experience that makes human life sweet just as much as it is human inter-dependence that maintains the stability of society.   At the summer camp there is the opportunity to demonstrate the simplicity of both of these truths in terms that are easily comprehensible.   The camp community is in many senses a reproduction of primitive society where social truths are reduced to such simple forms as to be inescapable.   The practical and immediate values of the camp are apparent to all; this subtler significance should not be lost sight of.

CHAPTER VII

REAL OR PERMANENT BENEFITS

1. We come now to a consideration of the real or permanent benefits of settlement activity. I do not use the word real to imply in any sense that it is of no real benefit to help the poor man. It is not real in that it is a makeshift. The ideal settlement looks beyond the struggling and oppressed proletariat. It idealizes democracy. It is convinced not only of the ultimate necessity but of the possibility of that democracy. Again, to use Miss Addams' words: "English and American Settlements unite in a desire to minimize their activities as rapidly as other agencies will carry them on. . . . A settlement must always hold its activities in the hollow of its hand, ready and glad to throw them away. It must daily live to die, and that settlement may indeed be proud which is able to say, 'This neighborhood no longer needs that kind of help, because its own civic and moral energy is aroused.'"

Jacob A. Riis shared this view. He even went so far as to say that the settlement should gradually drop out of existence, because the institutionalizing of social work marked only a transitional phase of our development. But Mr. Riis was an optimist; he believed that a problem once solved, was solved forever.

2. Were it not for the fact that the individual

comes into society an infant, unclothed and uneducated, Mr. Riis' optimism might be justified, and society would be spared the perennial task of teaching "the A. B. C.'s of how to get along" to its rising generation. Society is eternal. It lives forever. The individual, however, is continually dying to have his place in the social organism taken by the newcomer. The greatest problem in fact, that confronts society, is to keep the newcomer up to the standard. The human individual is the heir of the ages, but this same human unit can receive his heritage only through education. It is here that our present system of education is lacking. The individual is taught some smattering of reading and writing, a little mathematics and, perhaps, a language and then he is left to guess what the heritage of the ages may be. Not an inkling of his relation to the whole of society is given him.

3. The medieval church preached a doctrine which diverted the individual from channels of thought which might lead him to relate himself to society as a whole. The early church taught the individual that the salvation of his individual soul was an end in itself, and since there seemed very little hope of such salvation here on earth, the church held out the attraction of a life in another world. Today we seem only at the beginning of a kind of education which attempts to relate the individual to society and which is beginning to teach that, whatever may be the life in the hereafter, the individual here in this world must first and always seek the social good. We have even today coined a phrase "Social Evangelism," which is significantly

descriptive of the part which the new religion is to play in the coming world of social movement.

4. The kind of education that is to give the individual an understanding of his relation to the whole, is not a philosophy which can be enunciated once and then allowed to shift for itself. The newcomers in society must be taught their "heritage of the ages." It is my belief that the settlement has a very real part to play in this new education. When I consider the strategic position which the settlement occupies I am convinced that it has only begun to come into its own. It may be able to abandon some of the functions which it has been forced to take up as palliatives, but the real vital forces moving toward social understanding and social education will for a long while require just such a human organization as a central means of approach to better understanding between the elements of society.

5. In a general classification, society as it exists today may be divided into four groups. (1) There is first that large group which has enjoyed all of the advantages which money and position can procure, including the advantage of "higher education," but which is composed of individuals entirely complacent and unquestioning, who are not sensitive of any social responsibility, and who naturally wish to enjoy to the full those advantages to which they have fallen heir. (2) Beneath this group is one still larger, composed of under-privileged individuals who look up to those, whose lot it has been to have more than they, and are humbly grateful for such bounties as they may win for favor or hire. There are many of these

individuals who wish to climb higher, in order that they may "enjoy more things," but they none of them have much of a conception of the position of their class in society nor would they as individuals generally care, provided that each might make his own individual lot happier. (3) The next group, however, though also composed of under-privileged persons, is made up of dynamic individuals, all of whom are conscious of the existence of social forces and social relations; indeed, the group itself might be said to be class conscious. The immediate desires of the individuals are varied. At one extreme are those who, violently indignant at the poverty and degradation in which the majority of men live, aim to tear down existing institutions. At the other extreme are those who are anxious to build up and to educate the great mass of their fellows so that "society as a whole" may be made better and fairer. (4) Finally there is a fourth group, smaller, perhaps, in number than any of the others. It is made up of individuals who are in a position to enjoy those privileges which come with the advantages of education, of travel and of a commanding position in society. The spirit of this group, however, differs from the spirit shown by the one first mentioned. The individuals are alive to a conception of society which recognizes that individual men and groups of men alike bear a fundamental relation to society as a whole. The privileged individuals of this group are conscious of their social responsibility.

In order to make this grouping clear I have drawn a diagram in which I have represented society in general as the area within the circumference of a circle.

Through this area I have drawn two lines which represent natural lines of division.[8]

THE SOCIAL QUADRANT

6. The horizontal line represents the division between the privileged and the under-privileged; those who have enjoyed advantages and those who have

---

[8] In no sense does the accompanying diagram represent the numerical size of the principal groups which I have denoted nor do the dividing lines draw hard and fast distinctions. The social quadrant has been invented because it seems to me to be an easy way to denote tendencies and their cross-relations.

not; the fortunate and the less fortunate; or, as so many name it, the division between the upper and the lower classes. I have called this dividing line the Line of Advantages or Privileges. It may serve to denote the material distinctions which exist between men.

7. In addition to this, however, men are divided according to their understanding of society. I have drawn a vertical line on the diagram to mark this division. It denotes a spiritual distinction. On the one side, there are those who are moved by a social conscience and a sense of social responsibility to their fellow men; on the other those who are principally influenced by the motive of self preservation and self development. On the one side, are those who are alive to social problems, on the other those who are apathetic. The division between the left and right may be said to mark the opposition of liberal to reactionary thought.

8. There has recently been so much misunderstanding of what is meant by the terms "social conscience" and "social responsibility," that I want to recite an incident from my own experience which amusingly typifies the tendency of an average educated woman of the upper right to misunderstand these terms. It was at an afternoon tea, I think. A lady known to be "interested in charities" was asked by an enthusiastic young girl if she had read the latest book. "It has such an illuminating title too, 'Your Part in Poverty.'" The lady had not read it. In fact she drew herself up, with what was almost a shrug of the shoulders, until her pearl earrings shook violently. This was what she said: "Your Part in Poverty, oh, indeed, what

have I to do with poverty?" and she turned away.
This, however, is no isolated case.   There are thousands of individuals who go through life with little
or no realization that what they do or do not do has
an effect upon any except themselves.

I once heard a young hostess, renowned for her
charming entertainments, say that she "thanked heaven
her father had earned his money honestly or else she
would have a terrible conscience."   It is difficult, indeed,
to keep fresh in one's memory the fact that oneself
and one's possessions are alike part of this world and
exist only as a part of the whole.   The possession of
wealth, even though it represents capital accumulated
according to the rules of the game, does not absolve
the possessor from responsibility to society for the
administration of the principal and the expenditure of
the interest.   The woman, who made her conscience
easy because she knew her father had been honest
and because she also thought that he had been fair,
had no realization whatsoever of her own social entity.
If she lived on income she was responsible first for
the fair administration of the business or industries
on whose earnings she lived.   If these derived excessive
earnings from sweated labor or labor hired for a bar-
gain price less than a reasonable standard of living
required, that woman was as surely living by the exploitation of her fellow men as though it were her
own deliberate action, and this entirely aside from
any consideration of how or when her original interest
in the business had been acquired.   I do not mean to
imply that it is wrong to live upon the earnings of
accumulated capital but I do mean to imply that it is

very wrong to live in ignorance of the relation one's personal income bears to the whole of the social organism.

9. It is right here that the settlement fills a permanent social need. It affords a meeting ground where those who have no consciousness of social responsibility may come to know individuals who have been less fortunate than they, and to understand some of the hardships which must be undergone and the problems faced by men and women who depend solely upon their daily wage for livelihood. There are few who fail to recognize an injustice, when it is revealed thus disinterestedly through the simple medium of the friendships which are made possible by residence at a settlement. A few days of open-hearted living in a tenement neighborhood is a wonderful tonic for the well-to-do person with a care-free conscience.

Let me give a concrete example. A young man of considerable wealth once filled his automobile with laughing young people who wanted "to go slumming." They were moved solely by the curiosity to see what it was like; they particularly wanted to see Chinatown because they thought it would be queer and different and had read that it might be just a little bit dangerous to go there in a luxurious automobile. The young man wanted to be obliging. During the course of the trip they passed a settlement and someone remarked that she had a friend living there. So they all piled out in evening clothes and great wraps. A dance was in progress. At first the party danced among themselves but before long the friend, who was a resident, paired them off with some of the neighborhood people.

The host of the automobile danced with a young girl who worked in a button factory and then with a stenographer who was earning twelve dollars a week. Then he talked with the residents, expressed an interest in the girls and surprise that they could dress so well on so little money and asked what kind of homes they came from. To his astonishment he learned that the girls came from the same block where he owned some houses. This awakened an interest because he had always imagined that the very lowest sort of people were his tenants.

Further investigation taught the young man that just such young girls lived in his own houses. He found the parents, for the most part, poor working people with large families. The mothers were dowdy and fat but with a certain amount of character in their faces which reminded him of Rembrandt's etchings. The fathers were dirty and appeared in the evening fagged out and listless, generally complaining of the cramped quarters and sometimes irritable. He found that both parents usually put all their hopes into their children, sometimes with a feeling that the young people were unappreciated by their employers, sometimes to the point of actually bragging of a boy at college or a son who had "become a doctor."

10. There is nothing unusual in the story of this chance visit to a settlement. I do not say that a human interest in his tenants might not have been awakened in this young landlord by another means, but I do say that the settlement furnished him immediately with something of which he had not suspected the need, namely, a human understanding and a natural social

relation with the actual people to whom he was economically related. I know that the social settlement has
a wonderful power to open the eyes of those who do
not know what it is to have a social conscience.

11. On the other hand there are many for whom
the social settlement holds out an attractive outlet for
their activities and seems to satisfy a very keenly felt
want. I refer to those people who have enjoyed
unusual privileges of education and environment and
who *are* conscious of their social responsibility. There
are many young men, and women too, who have had
the advantages of university training and residence,
who have been reared in the atmosphere of liberal-
mindedness and who have been stimulated by contact
with forwarded-looking teachers. Such young people
graduate from the colleges and go out into the world
with deep seated and burning ideals. They are immediately brought into contact with actual conditions the
historical significance of which they have studied.
These young people are, perhaps, impatient with the
masters whom they find administering judgments
socially and industrially in the way that such judgments
have been administered for years before. But the
young people are told that they must wait, that they
must "learn the way of the world." They find themselves impotent and their ideals a loadstone about
their necks. There are plenty who drop the loadstone
and conform.

But there are those who do not. There are many
who demand an "outlet for their active faculties" and
who insist on playing not only a part but a useful
part in society. The settlement offers to those a place

of residence and a social atmosphere, which offers a
ready means of approach to many different spheres
of life. It offers, as a young banker, who had gone
to live in a settlement, once told me, a place where he
could "meet a few fellows who had never heard of
J. P. Morgan and who weren't trying to dress like
King Edward."

12. The settlement, however, offers more than an
insight into the many ways in which the "other fellow
lives." It offers an opportunity to put life to the
test. I think that Miss MacColl of Christodora House
has given especial expression to this. She was convinced that her education had been given to her for
a more fundamental purpose than as a set of rules
for parlor behavior. She believed that, if education
and Christianity were meant for anything at all, they
were meant to be used in the contacts of everyday
life and social intercourse. The social settlement does
offer the chance to live one's life and put fundamental
things into practice. Life in a tenement district is
reduced to essentials. Education and character become
not ornaments but limbs. Constantly, opportunities
are presented which demand participation in the social
movement and which call for the assumption of social
responsibilities. One lives in a consciousness of the
mutual interdependence of the different parts of the
social structure.

13. The settlement is the best agency yet devised
for the improvement of the social structure because it
is the most human. It does not have to wait for any
automatic breakdown of capitalism nor for any general
strike. While its aim is social it is a movement of

individuals. It is the only method yet devised which takes into consideration both ends of society.

14. Life in a tenement neighborhood brings one directly into contact with a great mass of men who have had barely the first rudiments of what is called "the advantages of education and good breeding" but who are still sensitive to the existence of the phenomenon which we term "society." These men come from the lower left social group. Generally, when the man with little education awakens to the fact that his own relation to society is controlled by forces bearing a definite relation to the parts which other men and groups of men play, he first becomes obsessed by the realization of the very undesirable position which he himself occupies. The only hope, which such a man can see, lies in his combination with other men in similar circumstances *against* men who are apparently living in the enjoyment of a more favorable social position. We have here the fundamental concept of the "class war"; the combination of one class of men against another. One will find factions among this group, all agreeing that, first and foremost, all hope for social betterment for the great masses of men rests in the possibility of victory over the property holding group. The points of difference between the various schools of reform; socialist, syndicalist, anarchist, and bolshevist alike, lie only in the means advocated for prosecuting the struggle.

15. Besides the radical groups, whose theories carry them to the point of preaching revolution, there are more conservative agencies of reform. There are the state socialists, who advocate the gradual assumption

by the state of the industries of greatest economic importance. There are also the guild socialists who emphasize the possibility of controlling industries from within by a sort of local government within each trade. The conception of the soviet is an attempt to apply local self government through the agency of industrial organization. In it the trades are represented but the unit is the locality.

16. The rise of the modern woman and the liberal reforms brought about by her demand for political as well as social and economic rights are significant of changing conditions. The growth of the movement has paralleled the rise to power of organized labor and has in a sense been related to it. Both movements have arisen through dissatisfaction with economic conditions. Both have been a combination within a class to procure more advantages and better living conditions. The labor movement, however, has had the misfortune to be composed almost entirely of persons whose position in society lies below the Line of Advantages. It has had to produce its own champions. It has suffered for leadership. The men, who compose it, have in general lacked a knowledge of any other social group than their own. Their horizon has with few exceptions been limited to making life more endurable.

17. The settlement offers to men of this type a chance for broadening their visions. By contact with leaders from the upper left social group, their consciousness, which is too often merely narrow "class consciousness" is awakened to a realization of the needs of society as a whole. I think that there is no greater service which the settlement can render than

this of ministering to the needs of the common man, who has risen to the point of intellectual questioning and revolt, basing his decision upon his own experience without an understanding of the problem of the whole. The social settlement can discover to him the existence of individuals who, though they come from another social group and have enjoyed privileges which have been denied to him, yet are one with him in spirit and who long for social justice. An understanding of this situation opens to the common man a concept of society and the social struggle as a fight, not between those who have and those who have not, but as a struggle for social justice between those who realize that the good of the social whole is the end sought, as opposed to those who are absolutely blind to all social interpretations. This is the ultimate battle of understanding with unreasoning personal greed. It is a spiritual battle, not a class war. In a sense it is the same battle which has been fought ever since the apostles went out preaching Christianity. We are only just beginning, however, to awake to the existence of social forces and to realize the importance of social as opposed to individual perfectibility.

Viewed in this light, the battle is to awaken the dormant side of society to a social consciousness. I have endeavored to emphasize the very real opportunity which the settlement has for service as interpreter of the new enlightenment. This opportunity, however, is narrow indeed, if only the immediate contacts of the settlement are considered. The settlement must extend its aid to individuals and groups which may become valuable forces in the social awakening. The settlement has, as I have said, done a great deal in this direction but I am convinced that, particularly here in America, we have not begun to realize what an active positive stimulus the settlement is capable of wielding.

18. The apathy and hopelessness of the mass of men must be overcome if society is to continue to grow. We have reached a limit today where further development at the top can count for little, unless it is to reach down, permeate the whole social body, and fertilize the barren lives, which the unrealized promise of modern science has left without a hope. The ordinary man must be stimulated to an understanding of his social value and filled with a conviction that such a thing as social justice is possible here in this world.

From where is this stimulus to come? I do not assume to pose as a prophet, but it is my conviction that it is to be a mass movement. I believe, indeed, that the movement is already well advanced. It is the new enlightenment; an awakening to a consciousness of social forces and of social needs. The greatest part in this movement is to be played by the forces of the lower left group. It is the ordinary man, awakened to his new conception of playing a social part, who will be able to rouse the apathetic and hopeless materialists of the lower right. In this undertaking there is going to be a great and distinct call for a new type of education. Our American settlements have too long neglected the opportunity to come to the assistance of the organized forces already moving in this direction. In America the settlement has done far less than it has in England to bring together those two vital forces which are useless, one without the other, namely, Education and the Labor Movement.

CHAPTER VIII

1. Having reached the conclusion that the settlement plays not only the transitory role of helping the less fortunate members of the community by direct aid but also occupies a strategic position in the scheme of society where it has the opportunity to be permanently useful, it is a point of necessity to inquire into the artificial relation of the settlement to the community. No organization can exist without a sound fiscal basis. The question, therefore, which is now before us, is to discover how society maintains the settlement.

2. At present, the settlement has risen very little above absolute dependence upon private philanthropic gifts. Most of these are in the form of annual or occasional doles. Little progress has been made in the direction that many of our great universities have pursued, that of building up great endowments for their maintenance in perpetuity. In fact settlement workers themselves have been by no means united as to the wisdom of attempting to follow the endowment method of finance. The peculiar urgency of most of the calls made upon the settlement precludes the hoarding of funds for a doubtful future use and demands the utilization of every means possible to make life as it exists today better and cleaner. It has not been

a difficult matter to enlist private individuals to give funds to be applied to the many immediate needs of the average neighborhood where a settlement may be located. When contributions are applied to the endowment fund, it means that the interest instead of the principal of the gift is made available for use.

3.   Settlements have been growing, however.   The mere maintenance of the physical plant and the payment of the salaries of the necessary professional workers have come to require an annual expenditure which taxes the limitations of individual giving.   In addition to the maintenance of a standard the settlement is, as we have already pointed out, constantly called upon to take up new things and to exert itself also from time to time to fill special needs.   In the ideal, of course, society should provide for the needs of its members as they arise.   But these needs, and the unfortunate circumstances which demand the settlement's aid arise because society falls short of the ideal.   I agree at the outset that the settlement is but a makeshift in so far as it ministers to these immediate needs, but makeshift though it may be, it is the best that we have and certainly the most human. It is one that enlists the sympathies of the neighborhood after it has come to understand that the workers at the settlement are open minded as well as open handed.

4.   The neighborhood too is generally very ready to come open handedly to the aid of the settlement. I have met men who contend that the entire financial support of the settlement should come out of the neighborhood which it serves.   There is at least one house,

the School Settlement, in Brooklyn, N. Y., where such a policy has been put into practice. In 1920-21, out of a budget of about seven thousand dollars, fifty per cent was raised by the house council. I know of several cases where sums equally large have been contributed by the neighborhood. Where the budget of the house is small the neighborhood is capable of contributing an appreciable percentage of the total. Where the budget of the house is large, the mistake is often made of disregarding the potential contribution of the neighborhood altogether or attaching so little importance to it that no effort is made to enlist its assistance. The University Settlement of New York is, perhaps, the most important settlement which counts upon its neighbors for any appreciable amount of support, and even here the greater amount still comes from "uptown subscribers."

5. As against the theory that the neighborhood should undertake the entire support of the settlement, I want to register a decided negative. The very fact that a neighborhood needs a settlement implies a condition where there are many who suffer and who are in need. It is not their immediate neighbors but society as a whole that is responsible for the incapacity of these to win a position of economic self-dependence. It is the obligation of society as a whole to help them into a position of self respect and self maintenance. There are three directions from which the necessary financial support may come: 1, the state or municipality; 2, industry; or 3, individual philanthropy.

6. It is true that the municipality has the resources; but are they applicable? The settlement has stood as

the pioneer in the social movement; it has been experimental; it has been personal. Success in the settlement has prompted the city to take up many new activities and apply them in its schools and recreation centers, its hospitals, its lodging houses, and indeed in its health, correctional, and police departments. These represent the activities, which, as Miss Addams so well puts it, the Settlement must stand ready to hand over, to leave behind. Were the municipality to stand as its financial sponsor, the settlement would lose its freedom of action and policy, thus becoming a fixed and finite institution, immobile and unplastic. There would be no longer an incentive to follow new lines; the state cannot afford to originate. It reduces its mode of procedure to a set of rules. The very value of the settlement would be gone.

7. When it is necessary to come to the assistance of men of the working class it implies that there is something lacking in our industrial adjustment. We stand upon the assumption that industry, in the ideal at least, should take care of its workers. Where the Settlement steps in to protect and help workers, whom industry fails to maintain regularly in a livable condition, it supplies something to industry. Industry thus owes a debt to the settlement. What sort of financial assistance, therefore, does industry give? There are cases where large concerns contribute very liberally to settlements located in their neighborhood in direct recognition of benefits to their workers. The City of Cambridge, Mass., is one that has worked up a system whereby the various industrial organizations make up an annual pool of their contributions which

is turned over to a committee to be divided among the various welfare organizations of the city.

On the other hand there are cases where professional social workers are employed directly by large manufacturing and mercantile houses to look after the welfare of their employes. Sometimes, through the organization of clubs, these social activities almost reach the level of settlements. It should be pointed out, however, that such cases are where the condition of the workers is better or at least higher than the average and accordingly where the need is least. It is with the workers in the sweated trades where the settlement is needed most for the very impetus and inspiration it is able to give that the workers may strive for better things. Where struggle is necessary we may count on scant financial support from industry. Indeed if support is given along social lines, it is with the idea of "keeping the hands contented" with "thinking and striving" strictly circumscribed. We have heard of many mills maintaining professional baseball teams which play for the edification of the hands—also free "movie shows," etc. Laudable as these efforts are, they must not be confused with the aims of the settlement. It is true that where industry looks out for its workers, as it is doing more and more among the better grades, the settlement becomes unnecessary. But where the settlement is necessary, which is in nine cases out of ten, industry is totally unfit to support it.

8. We are therefore thrown for our financial support upon philanthropy. This means that a large number of voluntary or semi-voluntary subscriptions must be counted upon and that some means must be

devised for administering the funds. The usual method is the board of managers or trustees in whom is vested the legal person of the house. Sometimes it is incorporated. Often it is not. Upon the board devolves the responsibility of paying the bills and maintaining the staff of professional residents along with the diversified activities.

9. No one can deny that it is the duty of the board to see that the money is well expended. The board, however, is made up very generally of non-residents; as a rule, through force of necessity, of persons of some financial standing and influence. Indeed the chief prerequisites for board members and, in some cases their only qualification for social service, is the money which they are able to contribute. Though board members are sure to be enthusiastic they are unlikely to have the knowledge and experience of the resident, and they are certain not to have the same view point.

Granted that these managers are willing and capable of raising money, the hope of success lies in the residents, those social workers and leaders who know conditions and can inspire confidence in those on whom the settlement depends for its financial support. It is a question just how much influence a board of managers should exert in the direction of affairs. It is not right that a powerful institution should be maintained in a neighborhood such as is capable of imposing upon it an outside standard over which the neighborhood itself has no control. It is not fair to subsidize a reactionary influence under the excuse that it is "charity."

10. The danger of reaction, however, is not so

great under private patronage as it would be if the whole of the settlement movement were maintained by the municipality. It is an advantage that each settlement is maintained independent of the others and is left to control its own policy. There is always a chance for new sparks of life where freedom is allowed. And freedom must be the byword with those who give. They cannot hope to control. I remember very distinctly the answer of a conscientious lady trustee to one of her fellow board members who was arguing for the independence from house control and regulation of one of the men's clubs meeting in a New York settlement. "But don't you see," she said, "that, if someone is not there at their meeting, if we are to allow them to run the whole thing themselves, it wouldn't be a settlement; we couldn't be responsible for what they might do." And very good advice it would have been too, had the club been composed of small children instead of thinking and aspiring men. The incident is well in point. It explains why so many Settlements deal principally with children and recreation seeking youth. There are hundreds of groups of men, and women too, who want only a place to meet, to get their balance, to discuss things. The settlement cannot afford to conduct itself on the lines of a nursery. It seems well, therefore, to urge most strongly that, however the money be given, it must be spent for the neighborhood. So far as possible, the settlement must be administered by the neighborhood or by those who understand neighborhood needs, spiritual as well as physical, and the relation which these needs bear to the larger world outside.

11.   Administration within the settlement is centered in the head worker.   Much depends upon the personality of the man or woman who occupies this position.   He must be above all a leader and one with infinite tact and breadth of vision.   The ability to see the other man's point of view is essential.   He must be able to deal with a board of managers, to inspire the workers under him and yet humbly to make the poor man his friend.   The very force of the headworker's personality is often an obstacle to simple neighborhood friendships.   Men live in awe of "the head."   It often takes a particular calamity or a great emotional experience to open the way, but such friendships are not impossible.

The policy of the house will inevitably be dictated by the head.   This often results in clashes within the circle of workers; especially where other strong personalities are trying to exert themselves.   Here is one of the problems that calls for the very greatest tact It is likely that some of the younger workers will be lead by their zeal and enthusiasm in wrong directions. The headworker must exercise the greatest care that he does not suppress individuality nor crush personality in his associates.   There is no more pitiful figure in social service work than a strong personality surrounded by mediocrities.   I attribute much of the success that has attended the work of Lillian Wald of the Henry Street Settlement to her ability to attract and keep with her strong personalities capable of leadership each in his own specialty.

12.   The personnel of the staff of workers is a constant and growing problem.   Is it to be a question

of what sort of workers the settlement can command or what sort of workers it can get? The pay is not good. Some settlements are compelled to take such resident workers as apply for "positions." They are not as a rule well prepared for the task before them. Even though they have passed safely through a course in "social science" or "philanthropy," they are not necessarily qualified to get into intimate social contact with the people of varying nationality, ages, and outlook, who live in the settlement neighborhood. The average professional worker has a tendency to specialize. He is likely to concentrate upon "boys' work" or to go in for "health work" or some particular phase of the whole problem. One of the settlement's principal tasks is to keep the artificial relation of these professionals to the community a human and natural relation. The assistant director of child hygiene for district X is an unrelated entity to the busy mother of six children; but Mr. Jones who lives at the settlement around the corner and told her what to do for little Sadie when she was ailing, is a friend of the family and a valued neighbor.

One of the most difficult tasks in settlement administration is the handling of the volunteer. It is difficult to enlist as well as to keep his interest. Because he is giving his services, it is not possible to hold him closely to task. It is possible, however, to awaken in him an understanding of his relation to the neighborhood, which if once fully comprehended will be a guiding force throughout his life.

13. Settlement administration, controlled as it is by the settlers and by the patrons, suffers because the

neighborhood has little or no voice in the direction of the policy of the house. It is true that the average neighborhood is not capable of originating and carrying out a definite constructive program, but it is not true that the neighborhood can do nothing toward that end. The effort is worth very nearly as much as the accomplishment. Social workers are prone to go ahead with their plans without troubling themselves very much about local initiative. Even where neighborhoods are well organized, self expression is a difficult thing. There is a tendency for bodies, which purport to be representative, to become cliquish. Among settlements that have come under my observation, Hudson Guild of New York has made the sincerest attempt to organize its neighborhood and to make it a vital factor in administration. The House Council is invested with some extraordinary powers as may be seen from the following articles which are quoted from its constitution:

"Article III, Sec. I—Powers of the Council:

To assign rooms, to apportion and collect house rents, to regulate inter-club affairs and the relation of the House with other neighborhood houses—to undertake and encourage improvements in the neighborhood, to establish a court in the house, to make house rules, to suspend or expel any club, to grant or take away the privileges from any club.

Article IV, Sec. I—Duties of the Headworker. He shall, from time to time, give information to the Council about the state of the House and recommend to its consideration such measures as he shall deem necessary and expedient—

Sec. II—The Council may at any time by a two-thirds vote impeach the Headworker;

Article VI, Sec. I—A new club may be admitted by the Council to the House and no club shall be considered a member of the House until it has been formally admitted by the Council."

It will be seen that absolute powers are given to the Council with regard to affairs within the House as well as the potential for activities in the neighborhood.

Sufficient power is given to over-ride the veto of the headworker upon matters of policy. It is a power which has been exercised. The right to impeach the headworker is unique. Although it has never been used, it is nevertheless a real power.

The Council on its part assumes a real share of the financial burden of the house, and undertakes the responsibility of underwriting certain items of the budget. The report of the Council's Treasurer for 1912 is significant:

RECEIPTS		DISBURSEMENTS	
Rents for Clubs	$1,194.46	Gas & Electricity	$ 992.20
Rummage sales and donations	334.30	Coal	495.50
Entertainment and Ball	1,090.52	Expense of Ball	65.00
		Repairs & Entertainment	944.97
	$2,619.28		
			$2,497.67
		Balance	$121.61

14. One of the most difficult of all tasks confronting the settlement is that of making both ends meet. In working over a great number of annual reports,

and comparing the sources of income as well as the purposes of expenditure, the special demands that are made and the fixed costs of mere house maintenance, one appreciates the difficulties confronting the budget makers. Where totals reach large proportions, it is to be noted that some attempt is usually made to separate fixed costs for maintenance from funds for special purposes but it is my belief that there is room for a great deal of improvement still. Such a separation, moreover, is not an easy task. Over and over again one will find the settlement running at a deficit and yet find a balance remaining in one or more of the special accounts. Often a need which is apparently great when the budget is made up is satisfied through other means. Sometimes a pressing need in a particular direction may demand the immediate expenditure of funds actually reserved for other ends. Sums set aside for house maintenance are often cut into in this way. Occasionally fixed expenses of maintenance may swallow up a disproportionate amount of the general contributions.

Funds for summer fresh air work are by all odds the easiest to raise, and yet it is the very form of settlement work which can be made nearest to self-supporting. One reason for this is that nothing facilitates the raising of money so much as the ability to show concretely where that money goes. It is my belief that, in the ideal at least, all settlement funds raised by contributions should go for special purposes or for "extension work." I believe that if settlements made a point of this and attempted to visualize their most immediate needs, giving the public the assurance that every cent went to put that particular work a step ahead, the public would be far readier to contribute.

Such a policy, however, would necessitate certain other reforms in administration and budget making. First, definite sources of income must be provided to cover maintenance and standardized work. Second, these costs must be reduced to the absolute minimum compatible with the maintenance of the standard. The old story of the chintz curtains and the window boxes is a case in point. It is difficult to convince a certain class of contributors that the house is in need of assistance, when they see that it is kept neat and clean and note that those minor details such as chintz and window boxes, which do so much to add quality and refinement, are regularly renewed. I know of one contributor, who discontinued his subscription to a certain settlement, because he said he could not afford flowers for his own home and he didn't propose to put his money into a general fund to buy window boxes for somebody else. It must be admitted that there is some justice in his criticism. I have merely used the chintz and the window boxes as symbols of those many questions of settlement expense which must be met in such a way as to prevent misunderstandings. A more definite classification of both receipts and expenditures, as well as a wider publicity for financial statements is imperative.

Although voluntary contributions are in most cases the principal, they are not by any means the only source of income. Almost all houses list among their receipts "dues from members." Sometimes this is divided into two items, "dues" and "dues for house membership." It implies, besides those who are actually using the facilities of the house, a class of people not necessarily "contributors," who are interested enough to belong to the organization. In many cases these dues represent neighborhood membership. Many houses follow the policy of inviting different "classes of membership," dubbing a member "contributing," "sustaining," "patron," "benefactor," or even "founder," according to the amount of cash that is turned over. Some houses make the mistake of going after the "big fellows" only. They lose not only the financial support, which amounts to a considerable total even though contributed in small amounts, but also a wider range of acquaintance and much valuable publicity. Small contributions, moreover, can more effectively be counted upon as regular. There is a positive danger where the financial stability of the settlement is based too greatly upon one or even a few large contributors. It means that such sources of supply may be shut off at any time by the defection of a single friend. It will then be well nigh impossible to find a single contributor ready and willing to assume the finite financial burden of the establishment, and certainly a matter of time before a circle of small contributors can be built up to carry the deficit. For this reason it seems to me a sounder policy to depend for fixed expenses upon dues paid regularly in small amounts and upon fixed sources of income such as rent, regularly chargeable fees, receipts from regular entertainments and activities, and, from income on endowment funds. On the other hand special activities, extension work, and emergency work may be carried by gifts for special purposes from larger contributors. In cases of this kind, there is far more chance of meeting the deficit by a special campaign for the particular form of emergency work concerned, if the gift be discontinued.

There is little doubt in my mind that settlements have not gone far enough in their effort to develop definite sources of income. The University Settlement of New York is somewhat better placed in this respect than the majority. For this reason I have thought it well to include here their summary of income and expenditure account for the year ending December 31st, 1919.

EXPENDITURE

Upkeep of Settlement House and Expenses of Administration	$18,284.35
Gymnasium Expenses	2,229.29
Social Work Expenses	3,823.32
Bathing Establishment Expenses	11,485.90
Summer Camp Expenses	6,579.26
	$42,402.12

INCOME

Dues, six classes of membership	$9,441.25
Donations	4,741.10
Rents, including banking space	5,275.10
Income from investments	1,320.00
Interest from Banks	39.50
Gymnasium Rental Fees	955.49
Fees from Public Bath Establishment	14,078.22
Summer Camp Income, Board, etc.	6,105.43
	$41,956.09
Deficit for the year	446.03
	$42,402.12

In striking contrast to the above is the statement of East Side House, Income for the year ending December 31st, 1920.

Contributions and other income $27,711.24
Donations to pay deficit of 1919 .... 13,137.13
Board of residents and guests at Camp 7,351.51
Proceeds of concert 1,460.00
Proceeds of clothing sales 7,073.37
Fees 5,696.49
House dues 341.70
Proceeds of raffle 595.00

Total Income $63,366.44

There is not room in these pages for detailed discussion of the classified items of either receipts or expenditures. In order, however, to give the lay reader some idea of the amount of money involved, I have thought well to include in one of the appendices a list of expenditures of typical houses.

CHAPTER IX

1. America has for years past been dependent upon European immigration for the recruiting of its labor supply. The foreigner has been called upon to do the cheapest, lowest and most unskilled grade of work. Situated as settlements are in industrial quarters, they are confronted by the problem of dealing not alone with the laborer and the many difficulties which he ordinarily encounters but of dealing with him as an immigrant beset by the additional difficulties which his removal to a strange country has forced upon him. The settlement is again and again called upon to be his wise counsellor and friend. It is essential therefore that one who would understand settlement relationships should have a working knowledge of the delicate problems of race differences and the assimilation of the immigrant.

2. In the United States approximately one-seventh of the total population is of foreign birth while over one-third is either of foreign birth or of foreign parentage.[*] In the twelve states of Massachusetts, Rhode Island, Connecticut, New York, New Jersey, Michigan, Wisconsin, Illinois, Minnesota, North Dakota, South Dakota, Montana and Utah over half of

---

[*] Census of 1910.

the population is either of foreign birth or of foreign parentage.' The foreign language population of the United States has been estimated at about one-fifth of the total or twenty millions. Of this number it is said approximately a half can best be reached through the means of their native tongue. At least three million of these have no understanding whatsoever of the English language.

3. The immigrant is in difficulties almost as soon as he lands in the country. Americans are not of one mind in the attitude which they take toward the foreigner. There are those who believe that the doors should be open because America is the land of the free and all men should be given equal opportunity to come here and avail themselves of its advantages. There are others who believe that a ready supply of cheap labor is necessary for industry and that immigration should be kept active so that a constant supply of labor may be always available. There are those on the other hand, who hate the foreigner and seek to exclude him; who even desire to send him back or to do anything to get rid of him; because as they declare, he is "ruining America." Recently there have been still others clamoring that the bars should be let down that the Chinese coolie should be admitted and the European kept out because, such is their contention, all European labor has become infested with the germ of bolshevism.

4. The average immigrant has been induced to come to the new world possibly through the promises of some enterprising steamship agent or influenced perhaps by the picture which has been painted for him

by one covertly in the employ of one of the large industrial concerns, of a land flowing with riches, where after a few years of effort one may retire in affluence. In all probability he will arrive heavily mortgaged by reason of advances for passage money. Unless he come at the behest of relatives already established or protected by previous assurances of employment at some particular point, he will generally find himself "dumped" in New York. Here without an understanding of the English language, with no knowledge of the nation or its customs but only hope, he will be crowded into a tenement district in quarters which are congested and often unfit for human habitation.

The immigrant is at the outset exposed to all the factional and political quarrels of which he has been the victim in the old country. He will find that many of the prejudices with which Europeans grow up have simply been transplanted to America. He will also be subjected to misunderstandings due to ignorance and inexperience brought about by close contact with people of another race with other customs, language and manners. That which is outside the average man's experience is incomprehensible to him and he either shuns it or fears it. The immigrant is no exception to this rule. The complexities of life in a tenement neighborhood with its contacts with other immigrant groups and customs are at the outset a distinct embarrassment to him.

5. In some of our western cities where living conditions are not so congested as in New York, the lot of the immigrant is likely to be a little better. Even

though he may make his first home in a tenement he will find the bulk of his countrymen living in small family houses and a similar home for himself will not be outside the bounds of his ambition. In the lesser cities the immigrant has far more of a chance to own property than in New York. He will be more able to pick and choose. He will take refuge from the strangeness of the new world among his own countrymen, with the result that we find large areas or, as one might say practically whole quarters in cities like Detroit and Cleveland populated by one race exclusively. This will mean that the customs, habits and manners as well as language are transplanted to America.

Though living conditions are better in the foreign born quarter made up of small family homes than in rotten congested tenements such as are the rule in New York, the foreigner will still face his greatest handicap. He will have practically no means for favorable contact with American life.

6. The average American usually looks down upon the immigrant, what ever his employment or skill, from a pinnacle of self satisfaction based on the hypothesis that he, the American, should always be paid more than the foreigner. The native born is quite ready to patronize the newcomer but always with emphasis on his own acknowledged social and industrial superiority. The "foreigner" is known by various uncomplimentary nicknames. He is called a "mick," a "dago," a "hunkie," a "polock," a "bohunk," or a "kike." He is frankly outside of the social horizon of the average American.

The latter, however, is a zealous supporter of the policy that has come to be known as Americanization. The ending of the Great War was followed by a furor of zeal to Americanize. This meant to the popular mind the curtailment of the foreign language press; the suppression of all radical utterances; indeed of all criticism of the government by the foreign born; the cramming of English down the foreigner's throat; and the deportation of all trouble makers or "bolshevists," as they were loosely called, who expressed any dissatisfaction with the established order of things. This wave of prejudice against the alien rose to such a pitch that there is no doubt but that justice was in many cases actually denied, and many innocent victims grouped under the blanket charge of being "agitators." A single misguided immigrant driven to blind despair and rage at the treatment he has received and the insults that have been heaped upon him can, by a single insult to the flag or a single act of violence, bring down upon all immigrants more distrust, more persecution, and more misunderstandings.

The settlements have come in for their share of criticism because of their sympathy with their foreign born neighbors and their insistence that they would tolerate no curtailment of American rights within their sphere of influence. Because of this stand, there have been those who have hurled at the settlements the charge that they were harborers of bolshevism, were pernicious, decadent, and un-American. (See appendix A). So high did this sort of feeling run in the period just following the close of the war that many settlement houses found themselves with very seriously diminished incomes because of the withdrawal of support, while it became comparatively easy to raise money for any new venture in Americanization work, especially if emphasis were placed on the teaching of English.

7. There can be no question but that it is a real help to the foreigner to learn English and it is safe to say that any effective program of Americanization should be built up around the learning of the English language as a beginning. It should be recognized, however, that teaching the language is not the end sought but merely one of the means to be employed. So far as young children are concerned, the teaching of English is made comparatively easy through classroom work in the schools and still more so by the daily contact of the foreign language speaking child with the great body of his English speaking companions both at school and in the streets.

8. For the alien parents the task is far more difficult. Unless the daily work of the father brings him into contact with native American life, there is very little opportunity open to him for learning English save classes in night school. The fatigue from his daily work and his natural reluctance to exert himself again after the day's work has been done make this means not only distasteful to him but also extremely difficult. Under the best conditions the learning of a language in a class is unsatisfactory and very generally ineffective. For the immigrant laborer fatigued from the day's work, even anxious as he is to speak English, the best that can be said is that it is possible for him to learn if he applies himself diligently. There are

cases, however, where learning through classes is an impossibility. The great steel strike of 1919 brought out the fact that some 50% of the workers in the industry worked a ten to thirteen hour day and one half of these seven days a week. Men have no time for night school under such a schedule.

The alien mother, as a general rule, simply does not learn English. Over and over again one hears, "no, we don't speak English at home on account of the mother." Living in a neighborhood surrounded by her own people, going out to shop at the small stands kept by her countrymen, and returning to her home and family, she has little call to learn the new language.

9. The conditions which I recite are typical of the tendencies and conditions which face the average settlement situated in an immigrant section. As an interpreter of America to the foreign born the settlement performs an immensely valuable work. Indeed, the relation which is possible in this case is typical of the best that lies in the settlement idea. Canon Barnett in his first London settlement sought to interpret the best that lay in life; its art, its education, its culture, its traditions, in terms comprehensible to the workingman. The American settlement is confronted by a still greater task. It must in addition be an interpreter between races.

At the outset there is the difficulty of language. Almost all settlements situated in a foreign language neighborhood either conduct classes in English themselves or co-operate with other organizations such as the schools or libraries where such classes are held.

It is my belief that mere classes are of very little value unless supplemented by social gatherings where the opportunity of speaking and hearing English spoken in a natural way is given. The settlement is well fitted to give assistance and by its manifold activities has the power of attracting the foreigner into a natural contact with American life.

10. But classes in English go only a very little way. They reach only a certain restricted number and type of immigrant. Many of our settlement workers have found it advisable to take up the study of foreign languages in order to be able to converse with the immigrant in his own tongue. Another way to the same end and one which is sure to bring sympathetic contact, is to have among the residents in the settlement at least one who is by birth a foreigner but who has become assimilated, possessing education and understanding of American institutions but with that rarer knowledge of the customs, ideals, and aspirations of his more recently arrived countrymen. Right here it might be said that I do not know of a single settlement but that has on its staff pitifully few equipped for this valuable work. I am taking into consideration the real assistance that can be rendered in this direction by volunteers.

We have only just come to realize the fact that the matured foreigner can be taught more effectively about America and its institutions if his own language be used. Even some of those who were in haste to destroy the foreign language newspaper have been forced to recognize its real educational value. The placing of foreign language translations of standard

American works in the circulating public libraries has been followed by an increased demand. The foreign born have a zest for absorbing a knowledge of the new country. Their demand for historical and philosophical works puts to shame the greediness of the native born for cheap fiction. It is the task of those who would help the new citizen to make it as easy as possible for him. They can stimulate the desire and direct perhaps, but they should leave the immigrant free to form his own conclusions.

11. Though settlements have been willing, they have been slow to co-operate with the organized work of the foreign language groups in this country. There are representatives in America of no less than thirty-five different tongues. The Bureau of Foreign Language Information Service of the American Red Cross reports that during the war there were in existence 67,000 organizations [10] representing the locals of 17 of these principal groups. These associations are making a great contribution toward Americanization. They are organizing schools as well as special classes and they are conducting a campaign of educational work with which the settlements would do well to co-operate.

There are many clubs organized among those foreign born who have had the advantages of American education which meet regularly with the avowed purpose of arousing their more recently arrived countrymen to avail themselves of the opportunities and privileges of American life. While consistently standing for the

[10] The practical suppression of the German and Russian organizations has in its effect reduced this figure to about 35,000.

study of American institutions, organizations of this type have performed a real service by seeking to foster the best traditions of the fatherland in art, music, literature and the handicrafts.

12. The desire of the educated immigrant to retain something of the old country is a natural race impulse born of the human desire to impress something of the individual upon society. The contribution which the foreigner is able to make to American life is too often overlooked, especially since the advent of the whirlwind Americanization propaganda. To keen minds, however, the value of the heritage of the immigrant has always been apparent. Back in 1908, Police Commissioner Bingham, addressing the annual meeting of the University Settlement, said:

"There is one thing about your work which seems to me extremely important. No doubt it has occurred to you all, and I have no doubt that you are working along these lines, but what has struck us over in Mulberry Street is, that in helping foreigners in our country certain precautions must be observed. . . . Let patience be the word, let tolerance be the word and charity. Don't be in too much of a hurry to make American citizens of the boys and girls who are growing up, I mean, to the forgetfulness of everything that is behind them and their forefathers. The Jewish race, the Yiddish-speaking people in this town, from various nations of Europe, all have behind them a race history, a national history, a literature, a development in art and literature, all of which should be honored and prized by them. So of the Italian, so of the French, so of other nations,—never mind. Take them as you find them. Graft the American spirit upon their own history and tradition, and in my judgment, and I am not alone in this, you will have more loyal Americans,— and then you will also to a large extent assist in not creating that idea of license, which is occasioned when liberty is suddenly given to a man who does not understand it as we do, and which brings home the idea that liberty is license. That is the great trouble we are confronted with here in New York, not so much real wickedness as a misunderstanding of the whole situation."

13. America has benefited from the contributions which immigrants have made to its national life to a degree which is very little appreciated. The first great wave of foreign speaking immigration following the European Revolutions of 1848, brought great numbers of Germans to the United States. They proved to be not only sound and practical men in industry but contributed to the improvement of American farming to an extent for which they have never been given credit. Even as late as 1910 the census figures reported that over 31% of all foreign born farmers in the United States were of German birth. Wendelin Grimm, who immigrated in 1857, brought with him the bag of seed which, with careful cultivation, was to make the Grimm Alfalfa one of the staple crops of the northwest. Another German, Carl Schurz, as Secretary of the Interior, 1877-1881, was the first to

urge the systematic protection and conservation of American forests.

The Scandinavian races have made a valuable contribution to the development of agriculture. They have located principally in the north central states, where they have been a factor in developing the co-operative movement among farmers. According to the last census over half of the farms in Minnesota and North Dakota were operated by foreign born; in Wisconsin 40%; while in Massachusetts, Connecticut and New Jersey about a quarter of the farms were worked by farmers of alien birth. The whole question of intensive farming has been greatly stimulated by immigration. The European peasant has been accustomed to doing only intensive farming at home because of the outworn condition of the soil. When he comes to America he instinctively applies intensive methods to the virgin soil, which has been so prodigally treated and so easily discarded by the native farmer.

14. In the arts and letters America has also received valuable contributions from the immigrant. American music drew its first great impetus from the devotion of German-Americans. The more recent wave of Italian immigration has brought renewed vigor to its development. The Italians have come the nearest to popularizing music in America. They have increased the number of concerts and have tried to make music the possession of the common man. The Russians and Bohemians have also made their contribution. One has only to read over the foreign sounding names on any orchestra list to be made aware of this.

Of late the Italians have made their influence felt

in sculpture and in the decorative arts. They have supplied besides common labor a goodly number of skilled artisans. In New York City there is an embryo Bohemian glass industry and a Russian brass industry. In literature too the foreign born have come to wield an influence. They are in especial evidence as contributors to the more serious type of periodical. Among the colleges the number of professorships held by Americans of foreign birth has been steadily increasing.

15.   There are those who see only an evil and a sign of decay in this weaving of foreign influence into the web of American life. Whether it is so or not, it is a force which has begun to operate and which nothing can stop. It is impossible within the scope of this volume to trace the gradations of foreign influence upon American society. I am attempting only to show that it exists and that it is inevitable. It is possible, however, in receiving the foreigner at the time when we acquaint him with our institutions, to relate him back to his own past and to seek from him some contribution of value to our society which he may bring with him from his own. I have attempted only to cite a few of the most obvious contributions that the foreigner has already made. It is my purpose principally to encourage those who are pessimistic to seek something better from the immigrant. Men give very largely what is expected of them. It is as true of the immigrant as of any others. Settlements are placed in a position where theirs is a vital opportunity to stimulate and keep alive inheritances, which when nurtured may prove to be contributions of social value.

16.   The linking of the immigrant to his past has

its value too as a stabilizing factor in all Americanization work.   I remember the pathos of an interview with a Jewish father who told me that the settlement had ruined his son.   And yet the settlement as well as his schooling had done for the boy just what Commissioner Bingham proposed.   It had tried to bring out of him what he had to give.   It had stimulated his intellect, encouraged him to take part in debates, lent him books in which he had learned of a life of which he wished to be a part.   In other words the mind of the Jew, always fine and intellectual, was liberated for expansion and usefulness.   But at home the boy was unruly, disrespectful and unmanageable.   Three little rooms up a flight of stairs that smelled of all creation, a large family, and a mother who spoke no English furnished little competition to the clean and exciting outside world.   It is the settlement role not only to reach the child but the family.   Nevertheless, where parents are slow and accustomed to old ways, even to hardship and to drudgery, it is difficult to reach them.   Then, just as in this case, they are unable to understand their own children.

17.   The pathos of the incident is typical of thousands of cases among immigrants yet it is not alone confined to them.   It is the desire of all American parents to have their children enjoy advantages which they could not themselves attain.   Yet it is a sad fact when the children realize that their life has gotten beyond the horizon which their parents are able to comprehend.   It is a positive danger where the children throw off all restraint and indulge "not in liberty but in license."   This is one of the problems of our modern

age, to balance the new understanding, the new facts, the new possibilities with substance. The settlement must help the immigrant and those who come to it to build foundations. This, however, does not mean circumscription nor reaction. The settlement must not be content to teach old fashioned rules of conduct. It must recognize the vitality in the new life and urge forward continually; but it must teach the new blood that institutions are but the expression of a need and that they must not be destroyed unless the need be removed, or other needs become greater, or unless some equivalent may be substituted.

"Produce and give—and, with all tolerance for the lesser vision of the fathers but with respect for their accomplishment—contribute!"

This should be the slogan of all programs for Americanization.

18. It has already been pointed out that favorable contact with American life is the surest and most evident means of Americanization. Of the immigrant family the children of course have the greater advantages. The mother, as has already been indicated, enjoys practically none. When the immigrant woman remains in the home, her life is isolated and remote from American influence. When she goes into industry, be the influence favorable or not, she is at least in contact with life *in* America. The immigrant man is always subjected to industrial contacts. His daily breadwinning calls him into competition with American labor either industrial or agricultural. It is a contact which is rich in possibilities. There are three factors

to be considered: First, there is the immigrant himself who is ignorant, illiterate, and unprepared even though he be willing. Second, there is the American laborer, who looks askance at the immigrant as one who would rob him of his birthright, one who is only fit for low work, and one who, as has already been said, is altogether beneath the native American's consideration. Third, there is the American employer. His relation to the immigrant while not evident or direct is full of subtle perplexities. It is a relationship into which it is necessary to inquire further at this point.

19.   To be perfectly frank, the attitude of the American employer toward immigrant labor is controlled practically entirely by whatever course is calculated to produce the greatest profit to himself. Policies, of course, are susceptible to change and vary with conditions. That day may not be far distant, however, when the American employer, will come to believe that many policies which may be immediately profitable are impolitic because of possible future maldevelopments. At present, one of the commonest attitudes which the employer takes is that of disinterestedness. It is nothing to him who works for him or how that man lives so long as the work is done. Such a policy will do for times when labor is cheap and plentiful but the moment it becomes scarce the cost of "hiring and firing" goes up and it is to the interest of the employer to "train" his men. Of course, policies will vary with the nature of the work. There are many cases however, where, ignorant labor is preferred. In many industries the skilled are in the minority and must be supplemented by a great body of unskilled

workers. An ignorant class of labor asks fewer questions and is content with less. Immigration has continued to supply American industry with such a class.

20. There is no doubt but that in spite of the contract labor law immigrants have been brought in on tacit agreements which violate its spirit. I quote from the report of the Commissioner General of Immigration for 1907 (p.p. 70-71):

> "The most distressing branch of alien contract-labor law violations is that which involves the use of what is commonly called the "padrone system"; for by this means not only is foreign labor introduced under contract or agreement, but often the laborers are mere boys and are practically enslaved by the padrones who effect their importation. This system is applied principally to youths of the Italian and Greek races, the boys being placed at hard labor, with long hours, under conditions wholly unsuited to their age, and subject to a wage arrangement which amounts practically to a system of blackmailing; in other words they are in effect owned by the men who advance the money and procure their immigration from Greece and Italy."

The padrone and peonage system has been used extensively to gather recruits for the lumber industry. It is practiced in Maine and in Minnesota and North Dakota. Under it the master has a secure hold over the laborer. If the latter tries to escape, he may be imprisoned or compelled to return until he has worked off the debt owed on account of the money advanced to him to allow him to immigrate.

21. The padrone system is not the only means used for procuring and keeping cheap labor. When large tracts of land are owned by employing companies, when the industry is conducted at isolated plants, at mines or remote lumber camps, we hear of the company or "closed" town. At the outset let it be said that the company town may be so administered that, though paternalistic, it may be physically beneficial to the workman. One who doubts the possibility of this need only investigate Port Sunlight in England, the home of the famous Lever Bros. Soap. There are cases, however, where the company's power is not so beneficially used.

Complete ownership of land gives a great advantage to the company. The protection of its property rights may involve such a paramount exercise of authority that the existence of any other rights may be altogether neglected, or even denied, where their exercise might tend to jeopardize the larger dominant property interest. Fear and shortsightedness are responsible for such conditions. To be conscious that they exist, one has only to note the general slurs which are handed out to men and women who have attempted to do welfare work in industrial communities. The charge has generally been, that such people are "busy bodies," and "agitators"; that they do a great harm by stirring up "discontent." The inference is that immigrants of the common labor class prefer to live in dirt and squalor until some agitator comes along and puts foolish ideas in their heads. It is very easy to agitate; it is very difficult to build. There are plenty of agitators of the type who incite men for the love of being followed and who are unbalanced by the spell of leadership. Employers make their mistake when they fail to distinguish the destructive from the constructive type. The former may be said to incite his followers to "rise and take"; the latter to "learn and do." Both types have their place in social history. When the door is closed to all constructive work, it is an invitation to the destructive type. Social workers actually have been barred from closed or company towns. Settlements have been looked askance at and their workers criticized for meddling in other peoples' business. Labor leaders have had technical charges preferred against them in order to get rid of them.

22. Undoubtedly the selfish motive is prevalent in much of this opposition to so-called welfare work, but it is my belief that it is in greater measure due to shortsightedness, fear, and lack of understanding on the part of the employer. I stress this point here because the attitude and point of view of the employer must be understood by those who have the desire to help in the great task of the Americanization of the common labor type of immigrant. The settlement has a background and a method of approach which should be of invaluable service in bridging the difficulties and misunderstandings between ignorant immigrant labor and its employer.

23. Slow as is the process of assimilation of the foreign born into American life, we have already arrived at a point where we are conscious of certain tendencies. The race rivalries and misunderstandings, which are apparent at first, certainly diminish in in-

tensity as the immigrant learns the language and customs of the United States. Among the better class of immigrants this process is more rapid. It is where groups of foreign born live in isolation under squalid and unfavorable conditions that prejudices persist the longest. In other words, with education and with the growth of a common interest, race rivalries and hatreds tend to die out altogether.

24. In Europe nationality has been built up and preserved by an insistence on racial differences and the domination of racial prejudices within limited localities. Indeed race prejudices have been the means used by parties in power to rally their nationals to their support whenever public indignation or distrust of the government has risen to a threatening point. By this means it has been possible to divert attention from local and economic issues and even to deny elementary rights if it be avowed that the government's purpose therein is to serve the state. Disgust with this sort of tactics, of which they have been the victims, has filled the European peasant and laborer with distrust of governments in general. They have had before them, however, the vision of a democracy across the water in America. Their traditional concept of the United States has been based upon a literal interpretation of the Constitution and of the Declaration of Independence. In their minds Americans have pledged themselves to these principles and have put that pledge upon paper.

25. Notwithstanding the differences between guarantees of liberty in theory and in practice which are so frequently a source of disappointment to the immi-

grant from Europe, in America we have found a community of interest and a common purpose stronger than loyalty to race. Nationality is bounded neither by lines of locality nor by lines of race. In the great size of the United States and in the diversity of races which compose its population, the influences which have shaped European development have been lost sight of in the greater dominating "society of the nation." So huge and so self-contained are the United States that, more than anywhere else in the world, is it possible to think of the nation as society. The United States is probably the largest political unit which may be called a social entity. Certainly at the present writing it is doubtful whether Russia may be called either a social or a political entity. The British Empire on the other hand, while it undoubtedly is a political, is certainly not in any sense a social entity.

26. Despite its heterogeneous make-up the United States has demonstrated its social entity. Before America was drawn into the late war, pro-German sympathies were widely and openly expressed. When it became finally evident that the German government would consider none except German rights and when the United States threw all its resources on the side of the Allies for the maintenance of the reign of law between nations, practically to a man the German born population of the United States came forward in support of their adopted country.

It would be ridiculous to assume that this loyalty was the result of a conscious recognition of the superiority of a nation organized upon social as opposed to racial lines. I do not believe that, if such a thought found expression, it was felt by more than a very few. Human beings in the mass act upon convictions felt and compelling rather than upon motives analyzed and expressed. ᐧ I am sensible that materialistic thought following the close of the war has sought to attribute all causes for action to practical and self-seeking ends and to discount the influence of ideals as mere "camouflage." To me the virtual unanimity of the mixed racial population of the United States in its participation in the war is an all powerful and significant fact. In spite of the advantage that was taken of the ignorant foreigner by many of the draft boards for compulsory service, where technicalities were made to count against him, the foreign born resident and particularly his family stood by the United States. The high aggregate of subscriptions to the Liberty Loans made in small amounts by the employees in industry throughout the country testify to the loyalty of the laboring classes. For detailed information of the part played by various immigrant groups in the war the reader is referred to Appendix C at the end of this volume. This participation was not all a result of compulsion. Unless the foreign born citizen had been stimulated by a deeply felt ideal, a belief that that which he held to be essential, was made possible by the United States, he could not have given such a full measure of his support.

27. Looking back over the whole problem of difference in race, which confronts the nation, we find that we have come to certain conclusions. It must be made easier for the foreign born to come into contact with American life and institutions. Advantage should be

taken of the use of his own language to help him more readily to learn about his adopted country. The foreign born should be called upon to contribute his share to the building of America. His own racial inheritance as well as his physical labor should be drawn upon and moulded into the society of the nation. In the ascendancy of the ideal of the United States, as a society of free individual groups and units, where race interests are lost sight of in the greater social interest, there is the hope of an end of race rivalries and hatreds, and of the growth of a new and greater society than the world has yet seen.

The foreign born newcomer must put something into that society and he will feel proud of his part in it. Just as the early colonists founded their New England in America into which they put the best of the ideals and traditions of their race, so must the more recent arrivals in contributing a part of their inheritance from their motherland found in America a beloved ancestral heritage for their children.

CHAPTER X

1. Beside the prejudices which still exist with regard to race, the prejudices of religion which have survived the age of intolerance are negligible indeed. There are, nevertheless, perplexing differences of religious opinion which are in many ways representative of the differences of race as well as the factional differences which have survived from the old country. The sacred place which religion holds in human life, the great body of tradition with which it is interwoven, and its relation to ethics and morals make questions which touch a man's religion exceedingly delicate to handle.

As a human agency the settlement is brought face to face with the problem of religion. As an agency which ministers to human needs it must have a definite religious policy. The settlement desires above all things to keep its breadth of sympathy. It is, therefore, impolitic to limit its religious activity to any one accepted channel of religious observance. Various sects with varying rites, customs and traditions have become so bound up with man's worship of God, that it has become difficult for men to unite in the adoration of the Infinite.

2. In the resolve to avoid the divisions which have

split the church, most settlement houses, including even those which are administered by churches, have declared themselves to be non-sectarian. Since all creeds are in the essential, interpretations which men give to their religious beliefs, it is difficult to interpret religion, especially to the young, if no one form of observance can be followed. Settlements have not been united in their policy in this regard. There are some who insist that some form of religious instruction should be given. The difficulty has been to reduce the form to essentials such as will give offense to no one.

Situated as settlements are in mixed neighborhoods they are brought into contact with representatives of all of the religious movements of the globe. Not only are there varieties of beliefs among those who profess to be Christians but Jew and Gentile are found huddled together in the same quarter. If the settlement gives religious instruction for one sect to the neglect of another it will mean that the house is going to limit its influence in the neighborhood to that one sect. Its very basis of existence, however, is for the avowed purpose of furnishing a meeting ground for all elements that make up the society of its neighborhood. It is impossible, therefore, to teach or espouse any cause that is not acceptable to all.

3. Greenwich House in New York City has spoken a very decided negative against the attempt on the part of settlements to do avowedly religious work. Even as expressed in the excellent little "Settlement Catechism," I think this attitude has given rise to

---

[21] See Appendix B.

considerable misconception." The average outsider is horrified to hear it said that the settlement has no time for religious instruction. This natural feeling is due more to misconception than anything else. When it is said that the settlement does not believe in religious work it does not mean that the settlement fails also to recognize that the same issue must be met in a moral problem. Because courses in religious instruction are not considered the most practical means for gaining the end sought one must not infer that no other method is employed. The settlement recognizes the love of one's fellow men as the first essential of human life but it holds of lesser importance the historical fact that it was Jesus Christ who declared that brotherly love was the word of God. The settlement holds that right living is the greatest moral force in the world and accordingly puts its emphasis on living rather than teaching morals.

Any one who has had any experience with boys' work should appreciate the truth of this. The growing boy is an outwardly unemotional creature and he is particularly averse to being told to be good. Critics of the religious side of settlement work are prone to forget the great moral influence of the club and the game. The same boy who sneers at the stuffiness of the class in religion will be the strongest upholder of the morals of his club and the ablest example of the ethics of sportsmanship. He will follow the leadership which inspires him and endeavor to live his own life according to the best ideals of leadership that he knows. The boy who actually lives these things has a vital living influence in straight dealing. He wants things done in the way he has been accustomed to think fair and right. He will put more force and conviction behind the requirements he exacts of others than the boy who has not had the advantage of direct contact with high standards of action such as the average boy's club affords.

4. There can be no doubt of the effectiveness of this method as opposed to the lip service of mere religious instruction, but there are those who require a definite outlet for their religious emotions in addition to the joy of living a clean and moral life. The settlement is, therefore, frequently obliged to furnish some form of religious observance which will satisfy this want. That there is an actual want seems to me very significant. It is the natural human craving for the infinite and for divine guidance. Some of the difficulties which are being encountered by the modern church seem to me, possibly, to be the result of undue insistence on religious observance at the outset on the part of an organization which has held itself aloof and detached from modern life. Where living is put first, reverence and a desire for an emotional outlet will follow naturally.

5. It is nevertheless a difficult and delicate task that the settlement faces when an attempt is made to minister to the religious requirements of its neighborhood. Susceptibilities, difference in forms of observance, and varying traditions make it impossible to adopt any single form of observance. It is my belief that, so far as the settlement is concerned, this difficulty has been a blessing, because it has forced the settlement to disregard the petty differences that have

so embarrassed and split the church and compelled it to go to essentials.

6.   Christodora House in New York City has met the problem which confronts it by going back to essentials.   The house is in its administration and support entirely Christian but it is situated in a locality where the majority are Jews.   Although its policy has always been non-religious, there still exists in the constantly changing neighborhood a suspicion as to what is being carried on, which centers in the very name of the house. With those who have become closely connected, this suspicion has become so far dispelled that there has been a call for some sort of religious service.   Every Sunday afternoon a children's hour is held.   The appeal is made through the medium of a heritage common to both Jew and Gentile.   The youngsters of the neighborhood gather to sing simple songs of general worship and to recite from the psalms.   An interesting question arises when the children feel themselves too old for the singing hour.   The boys are likely to cast it off altogether, drawing their moral stimulus from their club meetings and daily contact with the house.   The girls on the other hand require some more definite emotional outlet and practically, though not exclusively, for them a series of gospel meetings are held earlier in the afternoon.   Some results of these meetings are significant.   One girl overhearing a charge that the name of the house prejudiced the Jews of the neighborhood against it, declared that it was not so; that such a prejudice existed only among low Jews; and that the best Jews honored the name of Christ and respected his teachings.   I know of one club of

Jewish boys, which felt the need of going further than the meetings at the settlement house had carried them, whose members made it a practice one winter to attend a different church or synagogue every week in order to hear the best variety of opinion.

7. There is no institution, not even excepting the church, where the essential elemental Christian spirit is so dominant as in the settlement. The whole spirit of the work is so open-hearted, and so essentially is the doctrine "love thy neighbor as thyself" a part of it, that anyone coming into contact with the settlement is naturally influenced by its Christian spirit. Occasionally one will hear of a Jewish girl who has taken up Christianity. I do not believe that in general any conscious effort or pressure is brought to bear in cases of this kind and in my mind it is extremely dangerous practice to attempt to exert pressure. It is far more effective to graft Christian principles onto existing traditions. As the Jewish girl said, the best Jews are today recognizing the essentials of Christ's teaching.

It has been my privilege to observe the work in settlements administered by Christians; by Christians and Jews jointly; and in houses controlled entirely by Jews. Although in most cases there was little or no organized religious instruction given, there was apparent, even in the Jewish houses, a dominating Christian spirit. The lip service of mere religious instruction is negligible for its value as a compelling moral force when brought into comparison with the actual living of Christianity. To such a mode of life the settlement method opens the way with its direct contacts and its ability to arrive at an understanding of

the hopes and aspirations of *all* of one's fellow men.
To understand one's neighbors is to love them.

It was this Christian desire to so order one's life
as to make it possible to love one's fellow men which
originally created the settlement movement and which
still keeps it alive today.   Is not the growing recognition of the value of this spirit, whether it is called by
the name Christianity or not, by both Jew and Gentile
a significant and hopeful fact?   Does it not mean that
we are actually drawing nearer to the truly worth-
while Christianity, the Christianity of practice divested
of dogmatic considerations?

8.   So convinced am I of the truth of the new
awakening, that I can not refrain from a short historical digression at this point which, I hope, will serve
to clarify the steps in the gradual progressive development which the human race has been constantly making
towards this goal.

Some of our modern enthusiasms for the poetic
beauties of the mythology of ancient Greece and Rome
cause many to think of this mythology rather than the
late philosophy as the religion of ancient times.   Mythology, however, was only the first beginnings.   Greek
philosophy has a long and important history.   The
outstanding figure is Socrates.   Too much emphasis
cannot be put upon the influence which his life and
his teachings had over the morals of the ancient world.
The writings of Plato, who expanded and to some
degree may be said to have popularized the philosophy
of his master, influenced thought in all countries border-
ing on the Mediterranean Sea.   At the time of Christ,
Rome was the political master of the world.   The

highest type of thought of the day was embodied in
Stoicism. It was concerned less with the deity than
with human virtue. Birth, wealth, and even race were
held to be accidents of position; virtue alone made one
man superior to another. As Rome became more cos-
mopolitan, the austerities of the early Roman school
were tempered by the humanities of the later Greek.
We can trace through the writings of Seneca, Dion
Chrysostom, and Epictetus the growth of this humanizing influence, until it flowered in the writings of Marcus
Aurelius in the idea of brotherly love and the world
brotherhood of man.

9. The influence of some of the minor schools
should not be lost sight of. The Cynics and Rhetoricians, played something of the rôle in the ancient world
that the monks and travelling friars did in later centuries. The Rhetoricians accustomed people to listening
to speakers at the street corner and in the market
place. The Pythagorean school put emphasis on self
examination. The deity was considered the center of
moral ideas. Personal holiness and even ecstacies were
conditions favorable to the comprehension of the divine.
Contemplation, seclusion and cultivation of the self as
exemplified by Anaxagoras were tendencies of the
school.

10. At Rome the presence of eastern slaves and
freedmen as well as contacts at first hand on the part
of the soldiery, had created a demand for the worship
of the mysterious gods of Egypt. Great religious
ceremonies were held in honor of Mythra, Isis, and
others. For these, chastity, abstinence, ablutions, and
long mysterious rites were considered a necessary

preparation. With the decadence of Rome, the city of Alexandria grew to be the intellectual center of the world. Here was located the greatest library of antiquity. Here also grew up a school of philosophy known as Neo-Platonism, which combined conformity to the doctrines of the later Stoics with the atmosphere and hereditary tendencies of the east. Here at Alexandria the thought of the Greco-Roman world came also into contact with Hebrew tradition. Philo, living at about the time of Christ, pointed out the similarities in the teachings of Plato and the laws of Moses and made an attempt to reconcile the two schools of thought. So great was this similarity that at a later time we find the Jew Aristobulus actually contending that the Hebrew books had been translated into Greek and been the source of inspiration to Socrates and Plato.

11. Christ began his teachings in a world where, though the great mass of men were swayed principally by religious emotions and form, there existed leading minds dominated by a fine moral philosophy. Under the influence of conflicting tendencies men were thirsting for a belief that could reconcile the essential truths that lay in all of them. Founded upon the monotheism of the Jewish faith but divested of its national limitations, Christianity echoed the spirit and aspiration of the times. It expanded the Platonic system of ethics and the Stoic example of the virtuous life, tempered by the later Aurelian conception of the brotherhood of man. Christ's philosophy was the flower of all human effort in philosophy. It became the religion of mankind. The *form* of worship, however, was greatly influenced by the reverential rites and religious forms

of Egypt which were the popular observances of the day.

12. To a world approaching political dissolution and distracted by hostile creeds and colliding philosophies, Christianity offered in the manner of the Jews, divine revelations, authenticated by emphasis on faith rather than upon reason. Civilization, accustomed to forms was not ready for a religion in the essence, The result was the growth of the medieval church. To win a people susceptible to the supernatural, great insistence was put by the early fathers upon the miracles of Christianity. Indeed, so popular were these miracles and so rapidly did the number of them increase beyond even the bounds of the credulity of the times, that the church was obliged to forbid the practice of miracles except by duly authorized functionaries. To win over converts from pagan worship, a long series of oracles and sayings of the sibyls prophesying the sufferings of Christ had been cited by the Patristic writers. It was not until the time of the Reformation that inconsistencies were pointed out which indicated that these writings could not possibly have been genuine. In 1649 the French Protestant Blondel denounced the whole series as deliberate and clumsy forgeries. Corruptions of this kind were typical of the early days of the church which was bent, as an organization, more upon securing political adherents than upon helping men to live according to the gospel of Christ.

13. The early opposition and the persecutions, which were met with, caused the church to emphasize the value of life in the hereafter and to offer absolution from sins in return for martyrdom. The results were

very baffling to the persecutors. It was impossible
to stamp out an enthusiasm which made men so ready
to die. This early passion for martyrdom, however,
was founded upon a belief that the end of the world
was very near at hand. As time went on the zeal for
martyrdom diminished but the church maintained its
hold over the individual by insistence on the importance
of the salvation of the soul. This grew more and more
to mean a personal salvation in a future world. Power
over the remission of sins continued to grow in importance and became largely responsible for church
ascendency in the middle ages. In return for gifts
and contributions, either directly for building purposes
or in fee for particular rites and masses, the church
sold salvation to its adherents. Acceptance of the
church as the divine mediator between man and God
was a first requirement. Riches poured into the church
coffers from those who desired mediation.

14. Even after the sweeping changes of the Reformation, the church, though divided, insisted upon
its position as the recipient and custodian of the divine
will. Christianity might have perished altogether had
not the organization of the early church kept the flame
alive and protected it from misinterpretation by insistence upon certain definite conformities. The revolt
of the Reformation, however, was inevitable as reviving
learning made continued insistence upon the acceptance
of dogmatic facts more and more distasteful to educated minds. The controversy, which has waged for
centuries over these facts, has overshadowed the essential philosophy. The Jewish girl in the settlement,
who recognized the beauty of Christ's teachings and

the possibility of so ordering one's life, comes nearer to essentials than generations of churchmen who have disputed the doctrine of the Virgin birth.

15. Christ showed a way of life. The modern church does not hold in its keeping a body of complete and finished truths but it has before it a task to point out and teach that way of life. It is the problem of the coming generation to recognize both the necessity and the practicability of the way of life and to relegate to history and mythology those trappings and superstitions with which Christianity has been so long encumbered. As an organization the church has a larger task before it today than it has had at any period during its history. It has to deal not only with individuals but with social forces. Recently there has been an awakening among the clergy to a sense of the church's social responsibility. The movement has been met by violent opposition, threatened curtailment of funds, and accusations that "the pulpit is becoming infested with bolshevism." The greatest enemies of the church are within itself, and are those who seek to limit its activities to making individual lives contented and comfortable. Today there is an open contest going on within the organization. If it is won by the reactionaries it will mean that the spiritual hope of the world is to pass from the church to some organization which is awake to the social needs and the social problems that confront it.

The growth of social understanding is putting a new incentive into correct human living. The salvation of the individual soul in a world of eternity has become relatively unimportant. Men today are willing to live through hell to serve their fellow men.   This conception of the social good as the end in life has come to be very definitely recognized.   Such an end has a far reaching regulatory effect upon conduct.   It is an unanswerable argument for a Christian way of life.   Correct human living is more effective the less talked about.   The settlement idea offers a method of living where one does not have to talk about religion or attempt to teach it, but simply to live one's life.

CHAPTER XI

1. From birth it takes from twenty to twenty-two years for the human body and mind to grow to maturity The individual must acquire for his own use knowledge of the experience of the human race. The acquisition of this knowledge is spread out over a term of years and for the active mind it is in reality never completed. It is not, however, a simple process. Beginning in the most elementary way with the education of the child and its training in simple tasks to fit it for daily contact with other human beings, the undertaking grows more complicated until we come to the researches of the scientist and the philosopher. Education may be defined as the process of the continuing renewal of knowledge of the race, or as the means by which Society's recent comers acquire the experience of those who have gone before.

This acquisition of knowledge may be through the natural contacts of life or through artificial or conscious contacts. An understanding of these processes and their functional relation to society is essential to an understanding of the problems of education,

2. The simplest form of natural contact is through shared experience. The child begins by imitating. It learns from things done in common with its parents.

145

It acquires language by associating sounds with objects, because it has heard a certain sound always associated with a certain object. The names of things are the first words that a child picks up. Words like "out" and "down" are soon acquired, however, because the child learns to associate them with very definite happenings through hearing these words repeated by the mother or nurse every time the happening occurs. It is not long before the child learns to express its own desire for the happening before it occurs by repeating the word which it learned to repeat when sharing the action with the mother. Learning to speak is the first milestone in the educational process.

3. Practically all manners are also acquired through the natural contacts of shared experience. Of course, the mother will tell the child to behave so and so; she may even command it; but the child will very soon forget what she has said. Daily contacts, however, with good manners will count. The child will enjoy doing what it has shared doing with somebody else. Not only this but the child will be quick to detect actions which do not measure up to those to which it has been accustomed. Thus not only habits but standards will be formed. There is much significance here. Manners have been sometimes called our "minor morals."

Tastes, preferences, and esthetics are also acquired first and foremost through shared experience and natural contacts. The human being is definitely related to its environment. It will require a continuation of those influences which it has shared and which have become a part of its life. It should be understood, however, that through association there is a revulsion as well as an attraction. Too much and at the wrong time, may nauseate the mind just as easily as the stomach.

4. So complicated are the experiences of the race that natural contacts cannot be depended upon to transmit all that is necessary to the rising generation. To quicken the process of learning various artificial means have been devised. The school is the most typical of these. It concentrates every effort upon transferring these past experiences of the race to the uninitiated. There are two distinct tasks encountered. The primary task is to teach the various systems or the means for getting an understanding. The secondary task is to give a meaning to the knowledge which is taught and to help the child to relate this body of knowledge to life. It is necessary, for example, for the child to learn to read and write before the book of history can be opened to him. It is necessary to acquire a knowledge of the system of the relations of numbers, in order to understand even the common-place inter-relations of everyday life. This first task of the school may be called the "lesson." It is the basic task of explaining first principles. Besides the "three R's" of reading, writing, and arithmetic, the school must prepare the child with an elementary knowledge of some of the particular sciences, physics, electricity, chemistry. There are in addition, certain trades, handicrafts, and vocations, wherein specific instruction can materially shorten the process of acquiring by shared experience. Indeed, vocational instruction is becoming so popular today that there are those

who claim that the aim of all schooling should be to prepare the individual to earn his living. The preparation of the individual for a place in society is undoubtedly an important function of the school, but it should not be confused with nor limited to the giving of lessons.

It is a very common mistake to use the word education in this restricted sense. Neither is all the educational value of the school limited to the giving of lessons nor, it should be remembered, is the school by any means the only educational power.

5. The school itself has a secondary function. At the same time that lessons are given it is possible to give the instruction in such a way that the pupil, besides acquiring a knowledge of certain systems of principles, acquires also a conception of their reason for being as well as a vision of their use and value to society. Secondary education, dealing with maturer children, aims to accomplish this. The school gets beyond the stage of lessons and enters upon the period of study when the philosophical or speculative element enters into the instruction which is given. The *pupil* learns from the lesson to do what he is taught. The *student* learns from study to understand. Primary education disciplines the pupil's memory, secondary education awakens the student's mind. The former is drilled to learn, the latter must be inspired to study. One of the greatest faults with our educational system is the continued employment of primary methods throughout the whole course of schooling. Even the great universities codify certain selected volumes into a great alphabet which they offer to the preparatory schools

to be learned by heart as a test of the aptness of the pupil. Education does not seem to be able to shake off the bogey of the lesson.

6. Were it not for a certain other quality, a certain by-product, as it were, which our schools possess, their plight would be altogether hopeless. The schools are little associations of individuals and they are seething with natural contacts. No environment exists at once more democratic and more social than the school. At home life may be circumscribed and unrelated to the great outside world. At school the poorest child may find himself beside the child of the rich grocer at the corner, grovelling before the unnecessary dullness and inexplicable mysteries of geography, but alike thrilled by the physical accomplishment of the football field. At school young human beings learn at once their differences and their likenesses. So amid the welter of natural contacts and the discovery of democratic relationships, the preparation for life goes on despite the dullness of the lessons. The great majority learn to read and to write, to figure and to spell and to get along with other human beings.

7. Then sometimes there will be a delicate nature, one who will shrink from the jostlings of the crowd, one who for lack of happiness through ordinary shared enjoyment, will passionately seek to discover the meaning behind the lesson, craving something to love and to understand. Such a nature will learn to study, and will unfold its mind to grapple with the complex relationships of men and things gone by and things not yet understood. The school produces few of these. They are not all alike. There are those who in retire-

ment and detachment cling to their application to a particular task and so to a more or less degree serve the race.   There are those who, fired by the revelation and .inspiration of their own understanding, turn to their fellow men with a resolve to awaken in them a philosophy capable of carrying society to a higher plane.   Whether their vision be broad or narrow these serve the race as leaders.

8.   The great majority carry from the school those few formulas which are a necessary requisite of daily life and general philosophy of getting on with their fellow beings as they find them.   The average man goes through life with an increasing devotion to what he is pleased to call "practicality."   He insists that he has forgotten most of what he was taught at school and that he has acquired far more from experience. He is hostile to what he terms "theory" and he apparently holds the school somewhat to blame.   He is certain that to earn an honest living is the best and surely the most practical ambition that a man can have, but he thinks of the honest living more in terms of return to himself than in terms of production and its value to society.

9.   The school has given such a man in addition to his primary education valuable democratic contacts and a preparation for life as it is.   This preparation he has drawn from the spirit of his human environment in the school.   To many men it is the most valuable contribution which the school makes to their education. The spirit which I describe is always alive and always up to date.   It breathes the opportunism of life.

To what extent is this spirit made use of by the

directing forces in education? Is there not an unrealized potential lying dormant here? Is the failure in
general of secondary education to reach the student
in some way related to the undirected democratic spirit
which dominates the schools?

10.   I realize that these questions provoke sweeping
criticisms of an educational system to which we have
been devoted by long years of custom. I stand in no
position here to offer satisfying solutions. I can, however, contribute to an analysis of the problems in the
conviction that a clear understanding of the end sought
will prove the most fruitful soil from which constructive
thinking may develop that newer vision of education
of which we so sorely feel the need.

11.   At the beginning of this chapter the attempt
was made to explain the necessity for a quickening by
artificial means of the long process by which the individual acquires for his own use gleanings from the
past experience of the race. It has been already said
that the most typical of the artificial means employed
for this purpose is the school. Let us for the moment,
however, consider a simpler means, one where the
third element, that of democratic association, which is
so important in the school, is lacking. Let us assume
that, aside from its mother, the child is to depend for
its knowledge of past experience upon a single tutor.
It is likely that the child will acquire a thorough primary
education, perhaps a little more exact as to details than
that given in the schools. So far as secondary education is concerned the child will be influenced entirely
by attraction or repulsion derived from the opinions
of the tutor. The tutor may be a negative character

with no decided philosophy of life or he may have very
decided ideas in one direction or another. However
the case may be, it is easy to see the influence that is
in his power. It is one reason that there are so few
private tutors. Men do not want their children brought
up with decided ideas and preconceived philosophies
of life.

12. Turning back to the school, the potential power
to influence, which lies with the teacher, is not less but
greater than that which belongs to the tutor. There
is, however, a greater possibility of control. Through
the school board, parents can be reasonably sure that
the experience of the ages will be doled out to their
children only in such quantities and in such a manner
as they deem good for them. In other words, parents
and elders as a class consider it far better for instruction to be given according to prescribed lessons than
that the children should be encouraged to *study*
too soon. It has seemed best that certain definite
ideas which society has considered necessary or useful
should be presented in such a way as to be most impressive.

13. It was once considered expedient to teach that
bad little boys who took what didn't belong to them
went straight to perdition. The falling away from
medieval superstitions, however, has so served to
diminish the imminence of the terrors of hell that it
has been necessary to raise up the terrors of the police-
man and of the jail. Insistence upon swift punishment
for non-conformity to existing standards is undoubtedly
an effective means of discipline for very young and
unreasoning children, but it is my belief that it is

possible to teach even the very young the social need for respecting property rights. As soon as children are reasonable it should be possible to instruct them in such custom and law for which there is actually a social need. If social needs do not exist the custom is, in all probability, outworn and it is absurd to insist on further unnecessary conformity. Fear is only effective as a motive for conformity among the ignorant. Where there is intelligence it is imperative that the social need be made apparent.

14. As histories written for the young have portrayed it, the character of George Washington has been shorn of all human attributes except a tantalizing disposition to speak nothing but the truth, and a nondescript predestination to play the rôle of savior of his country. Undoubtedly the writers of such histories were firm in the conviction that it was best to give their young readers a portrayal of the character of Washington with the virtues drawn so clearly that it could not fail to stir in their minds thoughts only of emulation.

History as it has been written is replete with heroic examples of the struggles of patriots with oppressors. Indeed, patriotism has been portrayed as the dominating force throughout all history. Scant notice has been paid until recently to the economic forces swaying peoples, factions and classes. Where histories do pause to record a great invention they point only to its direct and obvious results without commenting upon the social dislocations and readjustments involved. Histories have been pitched in a political and military key with little understanding of the economic undertone.

And why? Because men have chosen to exercise a control over the giving of lessons and to emphasize the side that they believe best for the new generation to know. They have preferred to leave unsaid those things which reflected less credit upon mankind. History has been the most perverted of sciences but it has not been the only branch of learning that has suffered.

15. It was long contended that the world was flat and geographers who insisted that it was round were denounced as frauds and perverters of the truth even after Columbus discovered America. The great advance in astronomy at the time of the Renaissance brought upon its leading figures scorn and persecutions. The forces controlling education, backed by the churches, rose in a body to denounce the theory of the descent of man when it was put forward by Charles Darwin in the Nineteenth Century. The reason for the shortcomings of secondary education in our schools is not far to seek. It is a failure because of that timorous policy which aims to suppress rather than to develop. It is a failure because those entrusted with the direction and control of education grow fat on their jobs and seek to stabilize ideas. They fear lest new ideas creeping in may disturb the status quo and disarrange that social relationship under which the controlling faction has fattened and which they themselves feel it to their interest to maintain.

16. What then is the result? It is that schools, as we have developed them, fulfill the ends that are sought. But the end sought is not education. It is a mastery of the lesson. We are turning out from our

schools pupils who are masters of the exact science and the particular task. We have learned how to train specialists, but where our schools do not produce specialists the futility of so much that is taught is all the more apparent. The weakness of the system lies in the unrelatedness of the lesson to social life. There is no thought of a functional inter-relation of one branch of learning with another or, what is more important, with life itself. There is a lack of co-ordinating in the whole educational system. Where at present we are content to bring the human being to a point where he may hold his own in society, our failure lies in that we are not able so to relate his life to the mass of other human lives, past, present, and future, that he may be inspired and assisted to produce something for society.

17. I do not believe that I paint a vision impossible of accomplishment. The period in which we are living is one of an awakening to economic understanding. Hypocrisies and conceits which have held sway for centuries are going by the board. The growth of radicalism is but a sign of the times. When we consider, however, the consequences of a revolutionary overturn of our school system we realize that it is very like playing with dynamite to attempt any sudden reform. I am not certain whether the change will come by socializing the school and broadening it to a realization of its latent possibilities, or whether on the other hand the school will develop along its present lines by perfecting the machinery for giving lessons, while at the same time there will develop side by side with it another organization concerned primarily with the inter-

pretation of life and the inter-relation of its diverse complexities.

18. The settlement even as it exists today is able to fill a very decided want. It supplements the lessons of the school and tends to socialize education. Yet it does still more than that. Where the narrowness of the home fails to furnish an environment adequate to prepare the individual by material contacts for the complexities of society, the settlement can supplement the influence of the home. As Henry George has so well pointed out, very young children exhibit about equal ability in the primary schools no matter whether they come from homes of poor or rich, ignorant or intellectual. As the children progress, however, and the lessons become more complex requiring some sort of background of experience, that child, who is living in an atmosphere of intelligent contacts among people who can appreciate and help him to understand the significance of the lesson, will advance far more rapidly than the child whose home atmosphere is an intellectual void. Furthermore, if one of the children of an ignorant type of common laborer be taken at an early age from his limited environment and brought up in an atmosphere where natural contacts are the most favorable and highly developed, that child will develop in mental stature and capability beyond his brothers and sisters who have not had the same advantages of contact. I say this and believe it will be true even though the other children in the family have the same advantage of actual schooling that he is given. The point that I wish to emphasize is that the artificial contacts of the school are given vitality and meaning

only as they are related to the requirements of actual experience and the natural contacts of life. Where the home environment is limited and incapable of relating the individual to a full and useful life, the settlement is well equipped to supplement and broaden it.

19. The task which the settlement is able to perform here is twofold. It can actually supply the individual whose home is barren with an environment of intellectual contacts. In addition it can add vitality and meaning to the environment in which so many so-called educated people live, where knowledge seems unrelated to the essentials of life and is, in many cases, nothing more than purposeless dilettantism. There are thousands of intellectual homes in America today, where there is no understanding of any relation of the individual to the community, where culture is sought as a desirable form of personal plumage rather than as a key to the understanding of humanity. The settlement idea is dedicated to the creation of an understanding of the relation of the individual to society. The movement amounts, in fact, to an attempt to socialize education. When we come to consider the present effectiveness of settlement work in this direction, we are forced to admit that, important as the service is, it is altogether too limited in scope.

20. There are, of course, other agencies in existence which can assist in the task of socializing education but the part which they play is limited by a very general lack of conscious effort which is due in turn to the failure to appreciate the necessity of such effort. Organizations such as the Y. M. C. A. and Y. M. H. A. have built up splendid physical equipments, which they

have maintained for years, but it is only very recently that their work has come to show an understanding of what one might call "social values." In this awakening to the new consciousness of social relations the Y. W. C. A. has taken the lead. A type of leadership seems to have come to the front which is above contenting itself with the petty business of rescuing the individual, and which is striking out with the demand that society should be so organized that the individual is given the chance to grow and develop.

21. Even the church appears to be re-awakening to the realization that after all it does occupy a social position. The great report of the committee of investigation of the Interchurch World Movement upon the Steel Strike of 1919 breathes a vision and comprehension of social relationship and responsibilities which, if developed, will bring the church back as an active factor in daily life. It is to be lamented that so few of the individual churches have come forward in vigorous support of the Interchurch report. In the words of Cain "Am I my brother's keeper?" Churches that hold aloof, pursuing a negative policy make the same excuses as Cain.

22. The lessons given in the school are barren unless the primary teaching is supplemented by secondary education. The school as it exists today is not equipped to go very far beyond the first rudimentary task of the lesson. There are other organs existent capable of giving valuable and necessary aid. There is no full education without philosophy. *"Mens discendo alitur et cogitando."* The mind is nourished by learning but far more by thinking over what is

learned. The philosophy which a man forms determines his outlook on life and his understanding of his relation to his fellow men. It will be the directing force in his own life. It will be a part of his religion. Real education should carry men to the heights of original thinking and inspiration. But education like religion may easily be debased and stereotyped and "turned from its original office of elevating man into an instrument for keeping him down." The school must have the assistance of the home, the church, the settlement and of other organizations equipped to interpret life. Our present failures are not due alone to the shortcomings and limitations of the school but to the failure of these other social factors to co-ordinate. Above all the others, the settlement, comparatively recently organized and with its newer consciousness of social needs undimmed by standardization, should have the clearest vision and should stand forth as a leader to bulwark and supplement the work of the school. There is a great service to be performed. The great body of men and women who have had the advantage of the settlement point of view must not fail in this.

CHAPTER XII

1. There has been no humbler nor sincerer attempt to understand life than the settlement movement. A receptive and open mind has been a first prerequisite with the great body of men and women who have gone to live among the poor. As Miss Addams so well phrases it, the first aim of social workers "is to get into such natural relations with their neighbors that they can reveal to themselves and to the rest of the citizens the kind of life that exists in industrial neighborhoods, perfectly frank in regard to its limitations, but also noting that it has those fine qualities that the best human life exhibits everywhere."

2. This is not a task for amateurs. There is something more than openness of mind required. Courage is required besides humility. Experience and training are necessary. One must have had a broad contact with life in general before one can attempt to interpret effectively any single phase of life. I think that too narrow a background of actual experience has been the reason for much of the ineffective sentimentalism and lack of balance that has sometimes characterized settlement work. No one has recognized this more clearly than Jane Addams. "There is a tendency," she writes, "to grow so tolerant that some of us are afraid that the settlements are losing their sense of

discrimination.   Tolerance naturally results from a
closer acquaintance; and upon that we may well pride
ourselves, but we may fail to see distinctions and to
think we are tolerant when in reality we merely exhibit
confusion of mind."

3.   There are those who, when they go to live in an
industrial quarter, see only the suffering around them,
the inequalities, the injustices, the hardnesses of life.
They forget the life, from which they came and dis-
card the associations of an easier environment of
which they cannot help but feel somewhat ashamed.
They sometimes go so far as to cut themselves off
from former friendships which appear shallow indeed
in the light of the deeper experiences and sufferings
encountered in the industrial neighborhood.   There
are some who become more partisan, more bitter, more
destructive in their desires than even those whose parti-
sans they pretend to be.   But destructionists of this
type have cast half of their intelligence to the winds.
They exhibit only confusion of mind.

4.   Society is not simple and elemental but exceedingly complex.   Mere existence itself is so dependent
upon intricate inter-relations among men that organized
society will instinctively resist attempts to destroy its
system.   In an absolutely primitive society it was each
man for himself.   As population increased men were
compelled to depend one upon another and to associate.
"Mental power, which is the motor of social progress
is set free by association, which is what it may be more
properly called, an integration.   Society in this process
becomes more complex; its individuals more dependent
upon each other.   Occupations and functions are special-

ized. Instead of each man attempting to supply all of his wants, the various trades and industries are separated, one man acquires skill in one thing and another in another thing. So, too, of knowledge, the body of which constantly tends to become vaster than one man can grasp, and is separated into different parts, which different individuals acquire and pursue. . . . The lower the stage of social development, the more society resembles one of those lowest animal organisms which are without organ or limbs, and from which a part may be cut and yet live. The higher the stage of social development, the more society resembles those higher organisms in which functions and powers are specialized, and each member is vitally dependent upon the others."[12] "

5. It is difficult today for the man who holds even a humble position of administration to live the simple life. It is necessary that the brain worker be relieved of as many of his ordinary cares as possible that his mind may be free for concentration upon his real task in life. Such assistance is just and reasonable. But the "easy" life contains perplexities beyond the worker's understanding. The society which assists and supports its brainworkers for its service, is confused to find itself supporting others who appear to give scant return to society; whose claim to support may be that they have "always had it" or that they buy it.

6. It is not my purpose here to discuss the nature of wealth, its accumulation, or even the justice or injustice of it. The social worker, however is brought

---

[12] Henry George, "Progress and Poverty," Book X.

directly into contact with the problem and generally falls into the way of taking sides. To be surrounded daily by poverty and to feel its awful fatality arouses the sympathy of even the dilettante.

He who would be of real service must not allow his sympathies to unbalance him. He must be able to distinguish types of leadership, between, on the one side, Judge Gary, whose engrossment in the great game he is playing makes him blind to the fact that his pawns are human beings, and, on the other side, Thomas Mott Osborne whose essential love of his fellow men is the one dominating force that determines his actions. When one has played the game and won material success as Judge Gary has, there is a consciousness of achievement and a pride which it is difficult to penetrate with the understanding that there are those who have suffered needlessly, because no thought was taken of them.

7. Human nature is much the same always. Flattery and success are blinding forces. The men and women who give up the "easy life" to go to live in a tenement neighborhood may be as easily befuddled by conceit in their own success as the president of the greatest corporation. The resident in a settlement has too exclusive a contact with people who are not intellectually his equals. He receives altogether too much applause and admiration from people who look up to his greater intellectual capacity with wonder and amazement and hail him as a leader when in reality he only towers above them because he stands upon a foundation of advantageous early training and environment.

8.   Those who go to live in settlements should not turn their backs upon their former circles of contact. Even friendships which have grown apparently shallow and meaningless have a value.   On the one hand they bring the worker into direct relations with people brought up in an environment which tends to develop personality and personal force and where intellectual standards are uniformly higher than in neighborhoods where settlements are situated.   Such associations tend to keep the worker balanced and to develop his sense of values.   On the other hand they tend to deepen the sensibilities of those who have no active contacts outside the little circle in which they have been born and bred and sheltered and protected.

9.   Those who go to live in tenement neighborhoods have many difficulties which do not confront the so-called volunteer worker whose share in settlement activities is more occasional.   There is the danger of becoming too much absorbed and of enjoying too little personal recreation and too little intellectual refreshment.   The best work cannot be done by washed-out individuals.   Life, happiness and the joy of living are essentials.   The long evening hours and the demand for a maximum of mental effort at night make the life difficult and often, when proper precautions are not observed, really harmful.

10.   The low economic reward to the professional worker makes it practically impossible for him to marry and raise a family.   But the profession of social work is not one in which one can marry and settle down in comfort.   It is to the advantage of the profession that it is not so.   Very few men and women

are equipped by character and training to head a settlement. When they are found, however, their economic reward ought to be adequate because the headworker is responsible not alone for the continuous guiding policy of the house but also for the training of the individual members of the staff. Given an efficient headworker and a relatively large corps of day workers made up of both professionals and volunteers, in the ideal, the expenses for salaries ought to be divided among a limited number and more reliance should be placed on the volunteer. Where salaries are given and depended upon, those salaries ought to be adequate to attract and retain the very best people.

11. The difficulties and problems which beset the individual worker react not only upon his own character and personality but, where he allows enthusiasms to unbalance him or permits his own tasks to carry him too far in one direction, the results reflect unfavorably upon the whole settlement movement.

12. Quite recently, I was told by a neighborhood visitor that he approved of the settlement house and would come again because it stood for "culture" and the qualities that quicken the mind. This was direct recognition on the part of the neighborhood of some of those very tendencies which we have already discussed in an earlier chapter as functions of the settlement movement. Let us suppose for the moment that undue emphasis is placed here. To what end may this lead? Does a higher culture mean a higher morality? It may; but it does not of necessity follow. Care must be taken to avoid the danger of what is too often developed—namely a cheap veneer of culture. This

tendency is particularly noticeable in girls' work where we are likely to hear of clubs such as one of which a girl once told me: "We were organized to read Browning, you know, but the girls are so anxious to read a variety of authors so we are going to take up Austin Dobson next." Culture does not exist without understanding. Settlements are sometimes satisfied to give what is merely a smattering of the superficialities of culture of a type which is likely to breed discontent and emptiness of life.

13. There is another movement too which is sometimes spoken of as "bringing the beautiful to the people," which if persisted in without discretion and balance may be turned to very distinct harm. Masks and pageants, such as those which a few years ago swept over the country in a great series of performances and gave so much real pleasure and enjoyment, may, if indifferently done and wrongly insisted upon, bring only laughter and cheap sneers. Many may be thus alienated for whom protagonists would prepare the way for a better understanding and a wider appreciation of the beautiful. Legends of wonderland and stories of fairies play an important part in the development of the imagination of young children, but we can hardly expect that the same stories, even when dramatically portrayed, will arouse in their fathers any very vital emotion beyond a passing nod and an exclamation of "pretty, ain't they?" The actual must not be lost sight of in ecstasies of the imagination. I mention these things because they are all issues which are presented again and again within the settlement and wherein its influence may be made to count. Confusion

must not be allowed to grow by making life seem too unreal.

14. Again a very vital question is,—how far in recreation? Is there a limit? The crowded conditions, the cramped space, the attendant poverty and suffering, in industrial quarters do not imply that there can be too much happiness and laughter brought to them. The settlement is apt to be forced into competition with the already existing agencies of amusement, the dance hall, the cheap vaudeville, the moving picture show and until recently the saloon. The amusement provided by the settlement must not be constrained and stilted if it is to compete with these. And yet most decidedly there are limits. I have heard one authority on boys' work say that he had found it absolutely necessary to eliminate basketball; that he "believed it an invention of the devil" and that it absolutely demoralized a whole house. This position seems so absurd and untenable that we need not enter into discussion here. It does, however, illustrate a valuable point. It is perfectly possible that such an activity may overdevelop so as to destroy the balance in the house; this is also true of dancing, pool, boxing or any activity where keen interest and excitement are the attraction. Balance is the greatest essential of the settlement and it must be maintained if success is expected in anything at all which it undertakes.

15. It has been mentioned that there must be competition between the ordinary sources of amusement in the neighborhood and the settlement. This must not be construed to mean that such competition should be pushed or even allowed at all where the dance and

music halls, and even the moving picture shows are of such a character as to warrant the settlement in adding its stamp of approval. It is even possible to imagine co-operation. This indeed seems the best road to reform. If the settlement is to be regarded as the enemy of all amusement except that for which it is sponsor, its position must necessarily in time become untenable.

16. Then too there is the social worker whose nemesis is psychology. It is this type of worker who brings forth the criticism that the whole movement is actuated by excitement rather than sincerity. The human being is never so fallible as when vested with power. Intellectual power gained in the simple friendships of the settlement is one of the most amazing and one of the most easily abused. I have heard lectures upon, "How the Boy Reacts." I have heard residents discuss "what they could make their people do." There is a class of workers who find in the population of their neighborhoods material for psychological experiment. They are actually so dazzled by the excitement of the exercise that they come to think that the whole purpose of settlement work is to get "reactions" from young girls and boys or their less interesting parents. The danger that I point here is of psychological power wrongly used. I do not mean to belittle the accomplishments that are made possible by a correct understanding of psychology.

17. In the preceding chapters sufficient emphasis has been given to the caution that the settlement worker should not approach his task with the idea that he is trying to uplift those whom he does not consider as

good as himself. I want to refer to it again here because it is one of the first mistakes that the beginner is apt to make and one which is likely to destroy his usefulness altogether. Men are not capable of casting the mote out of their brothers eye before they have taken the beam from their own. This is equivalent to saying that men cannot make a success of uplifting and reforming their fellow men. The settlement idea was not inspired by a desire to reform or to uplift. It was conceived with a passion to understand. Let understanding be the goal. Love will follow and with love will come justice and righteous action.

CHAPTER XIII

1. There exists no panacea ready made for the cure
of human ills. Ready as men are to hope for the discovery of a miraculous formula for the deliverance of
the world from suffering and from misadjustments,
they are naturally suspicious of any new thing which
appears even unwittingly to assume the proportions
and aspect of a panacea. The settlement idea has been
misconstrued and has suffered for this very reason.

Canon Barnett was sure of his own aims. He was
conscious that his enthusiasm had attracted many vigorous supporters to his method, but he knew wherein
the movement had fallen short and wherein it had been
misunderstood. "I have written this paper," he wrote
in 1898, "believing that men do not understand the
settlement. There is as much good will today as there
was fourteen years ago; there is more knowledge. Men
and women, conscious of other needs, are more conscious that machinery fails. They are anxious to
avert the ills which threaten society and are ready
themselves to do their part. It is because settlements
seem to be a fad—an experiment of cranks or another
mechanical invention, that they keep aloof."

2. The many various activities of the settlement and
its organized system of work give it the aspect of

being an institution in the physical sense. In reality it is an institution in the spiritual sense only. It is not the form but the aim and the method that have given it its character. There are many who contend that it has served its usefulness and that it is already drifting into oblivion. The modern specialist in social work is apt to be particularly severe in his criticism. He is apt to forget the valuable contribution that the settlement has made to his own experience. Fortified by interest in his specialty, he is apt to get out of touch with the very people whom he pretends to serve. The settlement is continually active in introducing new friends to its neighborhood. It is very often the most direct and helpful means of introduction available. Its task is not done after it has introduced one or even a great many friends. So long as the neighborhood needs friends at all, the settlement must remain on the spot. It must be always ready and willing to serve those who seek an introduction or a point of contact with the great mass of their fellowmen. This permanent function of the settlement in relation to society I have discussed in some detail in an earlier chapter; what I desire to stress here, is a particular theoretic interpretation of this function.

3. Constantly throughout these pages, I have used the word "settlement" to describe a physical organization and a physical fact. It is not the settlement proper but the settlers that are of paramount importance. It is not the organization but the method that matters. The test of good settlement work is not the tangible benefit that is effected for the particular neighborhood, but the potential benefit to all human life from the

neighborhood spirit engendered. The settlement does not take its character from its gymnasium, its club rooms, its assembly hall, and its many physical attributes. The settlement itself is but the vehicle of an idea. A single room where human beings may see and know one another is as truly a settlement as is the best equipped up to date fire-proof building. As a room takes its character from the use to which it is put, so the settlement has taken its character from the neighborhood spirit which created it and which has put it to use.

4. I have used the term "neighborhood spirit" only after a great deal of thought and consideration. The term itself is paradoxical. One's neighbors are one's close associates, those with whom one comes constantly in contact and with whom it is a natural desire to live in peace and good will. In a general sense one's neighbor's interests are one's own. When I use the term "neighborhood spirit" I use it with the sense of applying the same treatment and interest to those who, in the natural course of things, would not be actually one's physical neighbors. It is difficult for the average man to realize his relatedness to beings whose daily lives apparently never cross his own. Neighborliness, however, is an attitude of mind. Upon the prairies, farmers separated by miles of monotonous wheat fields call one another neighbor. In the cities the use of the word came very near to being forgotten. It was the awakening of city bred men and women to a sense of the neighborhood spirit that created the instrument which is called the settlement. The recognition of a common interest and a common life shared

by people whose superficial lives and environments are widely separated is full of significance and hope for society.

5. There is nothing mysterious about such a concept. It is as simple as the profession of Christ that the first and last commandment is to love one's neighbor as one's self. There is, however, something very helpful added to it, something upon which the Christian church has laid very little emphasis and which was contributed to the world's philosophy through Plato, namely the concept of knowledge as a guide to virtue. It is my belief that Canon Barnett was mainly responsible for the reaffirmation of this doctrine. His life, his method and his work all affirm it. He sought to interpret men to one another and he founded his settlement only that men of widely differing circumstances might find a place to come together in mutual helpfulness and understanding. Too much emphasis cannot be placed upon the value of his vision and his achievement.

6. It has been many times pointed out to me, however, that the value of the settlement method itself may be overemphasized; that it is possible to make out of it a roseate dream altogether out of proportion to its actual limitations and without paying due consideration to those other social forces which are just as important. Cannon Barnett was the originator certainly, and the leader in a broad sense, of the settlement movement proper. He was only one, however, of the great number who put the idea into execution and have carried it far perhaps beyond the horizon of the original conception. It must be remembered

too that there have existed all along organized efforts of human endeavor which have striven diligently to make the world a better place to live in. Without the example of their accomplishments as well as of their shortcomings, the settlement would surely have succumbed to an early death. No human movement bursts full blown into flower. Martin Luther did not originate the Reformation nor was he the only leader, yet we are accustomed to think of him as perhaps the one man most typical of the movement. Long before, Canon Barnett conceived his idea of the social settlement there were men who had been moved by similar motives and had done similar things.

Yet the work of Canon Barnett is distinct and of greater significance than the work of this predecessors. The settlement movement, which developed from the work of the particular group of which he was the leader, differs very essentially from many of the movements which appear to have the same form. The "uplift motive" is NOT the dominating impulse in settlement work. This distinguishes the settlement, for instance, from the mission to which it bears perhaps a slight resemblance in some of the tasks which it undertakes. In Chapter IV the attempt was made to distinguish various points of view governing human endeavor. No matter what the viewpoint of the reformer, it must be recognized that his effort, his struggle and his method are of value for the light that they shed and for the accomplished performances which they offer as a guide to workers coming after.

7. The great economists of the eighteenth and nineteenth centuries pondered profoundly and wrote pon-

derously of the economic forces which they conceived
to be controlling the destiny of man. They believed
in the inflexibility of economic "law." Lassalle, Engels,
and Marx built up their philosophy of socialism upon
a foundation of economic necessity and the "iron law"
of wages. They saw no hope for society except in
the ultimate rebellion of the oppressed proletariat.
They saw no way for the improvement of economic
conditions under a capitalistic system and believed the
general social revolution to be a matter only of time.
The value of Marxian socialism to the world has been
variously interpreted. There still exist people today
who shudder at the mere mention of any kind of
socialism. For myself, I believe the writings of Karl
Marx to be of the very greatest historical value. In
the first place his criticism of economic conditions as
he found them was certainly just. Believing as he did
in the inflexibility of economic law, his prophecy, even
though fallacious, was altogether natural. His conclusions gave society a terrible scare. His method
taught men in greater numbers than ever before to
seek an economic system more endurable to live under.
In seeking another system, men are learning as time
progresses, that little by little, by constant effort and
by constant thought, it is possible to control and even
change through gradual evolution the operation of the
very economic law which was considered to be inflexi-
ble. The influence of socialism has been a healthy one.
Proclaimed as a political revolutionary doctrine, it has
brought so far political revolution only in a very limited
sense. It has, however, already brought about a revolution in methods of thought. With its program of a

reconstructed human society, it has given the inspiration for the quest of a society moulded according to human design.   It has given to humanity the inspiration that man can by conscious effort control his own destiny.

8.   The influence which socialism has had upon economics has given rise to a school of socio-economic thought which is based upon the recognition that economic tendencies can and must be controlled by social needs as interpreted by human reason.   The awakening of the mass of men to this realization will sound the death knell of narrow-mindedness.   Men must learn to lead that sort of life which will give them social understanding and they must not rest content with the pursuit of personal happiness and the attainment of their individual economic comfort. Social responsibilities must be fixed.   Social readjustment must be faced.   Social harmony must be sought for.

9.   The harm that is done in the world, the unconscious incipient harm is done by narrow men; men who do not understand; men whose horizon is limited to their own immediate needs.   More harm is done to society through ignorance than through any other cause. *The settlement idea developed from the preconceived conviction that social justice is possible only through complete social understanding.*   Understanding is possible only through knowledge, and knowledge may be achieved only through contact with existent social facts. The settlement idea is nothing more than the key to the situation.   The great movement of the day for social research is dependent upon the settlement method for much that it is able to accomplish.   The means of

approach is through similar channels even though few of the individual workers actually establish residence in a particular settlement house. Settlement work may be done without establishing residence. It may even be carried on in a neighborhood where there is no settlement house in existence. Broad acquaintance will, however, be necessary and this is made much easier where the entrée is gained either through personal residence or through the working centre of the settlement.

10. Men are governed by more or less irregularly defined motives in picking their place of residence. Sometimes it is the locality that they like, sometimes it is the neighbors. Under living conditions as they exist today, it often happens that a man's physical neighbors are in a spiritual sense not his neighbors at all. The settlement idea contemplates the selection of a place of residence in the spirit of neighborliness and the resolve to be both neighbor and friend to those who are actually one's physical neighbors. It is a motive just as simple and just as human as the motive of the man who goes and settles in a neighborhood because he likes the people who live there and wishes to be thought of and to think of himself as one of them. One man may pick his neighborhood because the neighbors are educated, or high class, or rich, another because the neighbors are human. The man who wishes to live among people who are just like himself or whom he wishes to imitate in order that he may be thought of as one of them is a narrow man. The man who longs for contact with people who are unlike himself is a broad man and one

who will grow in character and intellect from such contacts.

11.   To put the settlement idea into practice in its most elemental form one has first to become a settler, or, I might better say, an open-minded and open-hearted neighbor.   It is a comparatively easy thing to settle in a district where working people live, especially if one be endowed with the means to provide for oneself some of the more essential comforts of life.   It is not always as easy to win the respect and sympathetic understanding of one's neighbors.   Infinite patience is required.   Few men have an understanding of even the simplest human relationships and an intelligent understanding of group relationship is even more difficult to comprehend.   Education has not yet brought men to the point where they believe it necessary for the average individual to trouble himself about such problems.   When the settler attempts to uncover the social roots of his neighborhood he will be met with indifference and even resentment.   He will find that the average man prefers to slouch on a dirty stoop on an unkempt street and soothe his body with a little tobacco rather than to bother himself about his relation to society.   Some of the difficulties of "getting into touch" with apathetic neighbors have been discussed in a previous chapter.   They must be recognized and faced.

12.   To a great extent the entrée that is gained through the settlement house proper is of assistance in overcoming the barriers of both indifference and diffidence.   It must be remembered, however, that the direct influence of the settlement is limited to com-

paratively few people in the neighborhood. Only by the multiplication of spheres of contact of this type can the settlement method and influence be brought directly to the majority of men. It is foolhardy to talk of the multiplication on an adequate scale of settlement houses as they are organized today. With the settlement house as a center, however, it is to be hoped that residential communities of widening influence may grow in importance. The possibilities of individual personal residence as well as the possibilities of mere visits have as yet been but imperfectly realized. What is needed right now is not so much more settlements, as more living facilities in settlement neighborhoods where educated men and women may make their homes. What is needed most of all is a greater number of intelligent visitors, both regular and occasional, who will find in the settlement community the inspiration and the means to a broader social understanding, and who will be moved through the vision of social justice to apply conscious effort toward the improvement of human relationships.

13. Such in short is a citizen's duty. It calls for the broadening of the mind and for unlimited sympathies. It calls also for specialized thinking upon particular problems. In the collective mind of the settlement, the varied viewpoints of human thinking and human effort should be represented. I have referred to the lack of definite contact between American settlements and American labor organizations. Residence in the settlement of men charged with leadership in the labor movement is as necessary and as valuable to the community as is the presence of settlers from

another district.   That there are practically no such
residents, is one of the most serious charges that can
be brought against the settlement.   It is a defect for
which a remedy should be sought with all possible
breadth of vision.   It should be remembered that both
the settler and the neighborhood gain knowledge as
well as understanding from mutual contact.   No vital
force in the community should be unrepresented or
untouched by the collective life of the organized neighborhood.

14.   If the settlement is to carry on at all it must be
along these lines.   It will not be through institutionalizing but through popularizing the idea.   As a contribution to the solution of social problems the work of the
settlement has been invaluable for the *viewpoint* that
it has furnished.   It will continue to be so.   It has
proved to be a *method of approach,* the efficiency of
which is undoubted.   It is a method which has tended
to *allay suspicion* because it is founded upon *simple
friendship* and *trust in humanity.*   It seeks its knowledge with open mind in the spirit of humility.   It
stands convinced alike of the *possibility and the necessity of democracy.*   It advocates equal opportunity for
all.   It deprecates class distinctions and class limitations.   It makes use of class consciousness and group
consciousness only as a means of arousing the dulled
and senseless members of society to a consciousness
of their social entity and of awakening them to a
realization of group relationships to society as a whole.

The settlement idea contemplates the *ultimate comprehension by man of a complete social understanding.*
It is a goal which man may reasonably hope to attain.

But the unwieldy power of the great economic and social forces which dominate society can be mastered only by the continued application of a directing intelligence. Man must approach the task with his eyes open, with patience, and with a consciousness of his purpose. The task is the more difficult because no finite goal can be described which represents the attainment of the complete social understanding that is sought. Social theory, observation, and experiment must be tried out. I am aware that this essay is open to criticism because the conclusions that are drawn represent nothing which can be grasped as concrete by the many men who are ready and willing to see the problems of the universe settled tomorrow. Social understanding, however, is not a concrete thing. It certainly can not be attained unless man acquires knowledge of himself as a social being, of his social relationships to others, and of the relationships which himself, other individuals, and other groups of individuals bear to society as a whole. Contact with life is a first essential. From contact comes knowledge and from knowledge, understanding. It has not been my purpose to summarize a body of facts nor even to do justice to the knowledge of social conditions, which the settlement movement has done much to promote. The idea of the settlement is the key by which understanding of social phenomena may be obtained. It is a means of approach. It is not propaganda but a method. The vision of social justice is there but it is a distant vision. What I have written has been in the hope that by a more widespread and more intelligent application of the idea that distant vision may be brought nearer.

APPENDIX A

The following series of three statements were issued by the United Neighborhood Houses of New York during the period of reaction, questioning, and criticism following the close of the Great War.

No. 1

A SETTLEMENT SUMMARY

The Settlements stand for service through neighborhood co-operation. They have sought, for many years, to interpret the best in America to their foreign neighbors, and to cultivate for America all that those neighbors have brought to her of value. They have steadily worked to raise the ideals of life and to deepen spiritual values. They have served as interpreters between classes. They differ greatly in opinion and method. They unite in sympathy and common aims. They are working always for progress by orderly process of law and for an America in which all classes shall live and work in concord.

No. 2

WHAT THE SETTLEMENTS STAND FOR

The Settlements stand for service through neighborhood co-operation. The thing that distinguished the Settlements from other social undertakings was a desire to get a first-hand knowledge of the conditions of life and labor in the poorer sections of great cities. With this knowledge they sought to solve the problems through the co-operation of the people involved besides requisitioning all available resources. The Settlement does not come into a neighborhood with any preconceived social theory but with a determination to get at the facts and then develop a method of attack.

The aim of the Settlement is always the building of a better social life through the development of character in individuals and an improvement in the environment in which the individual life is lived.

The method of working towards this aim will differ with different Settlements but the aim is always the same. It is based upon respect for personality and is satisfied with nothing less than the opening of opportunity to all for the highest development, physically, morally, and spiritually, of which each is capable.

WHAT SETTLEMENTS HAVE DONE

While no two Settlements are exactly alike in method or in the character of the work they undertake there are certain features common to all.

1. A common meeting place: A Settlement is first of all a Home. It is composed of a resident group of socially minded persons who are eager to learn the problems which their neighbors face and to join with them in seeking the solution. They wish to be in friendly touch with all the elements in their neighborhood. They want the Settlement to be a common meeting place for people

of all sorts and conditions. They seek to overcome class and race prejudice and bring neighbors together as friends. They encourage each to bring his contribution to the common good and thus try to conserve the values that different races and social groups possess. In this way the foreign born often find a new appreciation for the cultured arts of their race. Coming in contact with many different groups, only vaguely understood by the older Americans, the Settlements frequently have served as an Interpreter.

2. A pioneer in social improvement: Many of the social activities now regarded as common-places of city administration were initiated in the Settlements. They were experiment stations where new proposals in education, recreation and public health work were tested. The first kindergartens were established in Settlements. The yards of these institutions were early used as playgrounds. The beginnings of medical inspection and school nursing, growing out of the experience of the Henry Street Settlement, offer a notable example of this pioneer work. The evils of dark, unsanitary tenements impressed themselves on the residents in the first Settlements who were among the early leaders in housing reform. It should never be forgotten that it was the Settlements which first realized the need and opportunity of neighborhood organization and blazed the way for more recent efforts to organize communities for social improvement.

3. As social centers: From the first the Settlements have offered facilities for social gatherings. When the saloons were about the only places which could be called social centers, the Settlements saw their opportunity of rendering a service to their neighborhood

by providing rooms where those who wished to gather for self-improvement along intellectual and social lines could meet. Out of their club work conducted on the principle of self-government have come important influences in developing a genuine spirit of democracy.

4. As centers of co-operation: It is in the Settlements that channels of local need and supply center. Neighbors in search of information on every conceivable topic, those in need of material help, those with personal problems to solve come to the Settlements as to "a big brother." Here they expect to find the help they need or information as to the source of supply. Thus the Settlements became neighborhood clearing houses. That they hold the confidence of large numbers was demonstrated during the war when they gave the approach to their neighborhoods for such government agencies as the Food and Fuel Administration. In neighborhoods where Settlements existed, the war time agencies turned naturally to these institutions to accomplish their purposes.

"A TREE IS KNOWN BY ITS FRUITS"

It would be possible to compile a long list of those who, having grown up under Settlement influences, are now occupying responsible positions in the life of this and other cities. Such a list would include doctors, lawyers, college professors, school teachers, many social workers, and leaders in movements for better municipal government.

Four Settlements in New York City are today directed by graduates of the University Settlement. In every walk of life one meets those who found inspiration and guidance in the Settlements and are now useful members of their communities.

Likewise from among those who have had the experience of residence in Settlements many today are filling positions of national importance as leaders in the political, educational, and religious life of the country and in the field of social reconstruction. These men and women gladly acknowledge the debt they owe to the Settlements for the human point of view they gained from their experience.

WHAT OF THE FUTURE

Such local neighborhood agencies as the Settlements are too valuable to be discarded. They have sunk their roots deep in the local soil. While it is conceivable and even probable that many of the activities they are carrying on will be turned over to municipal and community agencies, there will be need of such groups of intellectual, socially minded people living in crowded neighborhoods, and to some extent sharing the experiences of their neighbors, with the aim of organizing their neighbors for the improvement of local conditions, so long as conditions exist which need to be improved.

GAYLORD S. WHITE.

No. 3

IN RESPONSE TO QUESTIONS

In response to questions as to the attitude of the United Neighborhood Houses on Organized Charity, Industry, and Americanization, the Houses submit the following:

ORGANIZED CHARITY

We recognize organized charity as temporarily helpful and necessary. But we recognize also that private philanthropy must and should give way to a community self help. To that end, we dedicate our energies to replacing philanthropic agencies by public instruments, recognized by the people as creations of their own to solve their own difficulties.

INDUSTRY

We recognize that the present relationship of employer and employe is unsatisfactory and that readjustment must take place. Neither capital nor labor should possess arbitrary and autocratic control of industry. The present economic strife must give way to an orderly democratization of industry. The conditions of production should be such as to induce the worker to contribute to that production in the largest measure possible. It should insure to him and his family a proper share in the fruit of his labor. It must further secure to his children the same opportunities for their full share of happiness and for the development of their minds and bodies, as for the children of other classes. Such re-organization, further, must give full protection to legitimate capital and to the brains and talents required in conducting business.

On the other hand, we consider all efforts to minimize individual efficiency, or to reduce the possible maximum of production of a country, as destructive and inimical to the best interest both of the workers and of society.

The present exigencies of the entire world make wanton attempts on the part of either capital or labor to hold back or reduce production a crime against civilization.

AMERICANIZATION

The Settlements believe firmly in American governmental ideals and, in the 34 years since their founding, have been teaching a respect for them that is based on understanding. Through the example of the club work, there has grown up a conception of the orderly process of government that is far more impressive than any teaching by precept could possibly be. Rule by majority, the right of the minority to be heard, the evolutionary process of change, as taught and practiced in the club, becomes woven into the life and spirit of the young men and women who grow up in the Settlements. They gain a power to think for themselves that is the basis of a secure and intelligent democracy. The Settlements, having practiced rule by majority for so many years, have, in the firmest manner, shown their condemnation of class or partisan rule.

This is the process of Americanization. It means not only a better understanding of America by the immigrant but also a better understanding of the immigrant, in all his resources and his weakness, by America. This understanding must be as deep as friendship itself, and cannot be hastily reached by ready-made methods. It requires time. Americanization that expresses the best in our national life, involves the securing to the immigrant of good working conditions, fair wages, decent housing, health protection and recreational opportunity; leisure to learn to know, understand, and love our institutions. It means also a desire, on our part, to preserve and perfect all historical cultural and other contributions which our new citizens may have to make. It is idle to talk of "citizenship classes," "speak English" drives, or other mechanical devices, unless these efforts are vitalized by the determination of Americans to welcome the newcomer with the offer of justice and opportunity.

Such a course makes of men and women good neighbors and responsible citizens. It puts life in a community on a family basis. It brings government very near and makes of it a living, understandable thing, friendly, and daily serviceable to the thousand needs of our people.

THE UNITED NEIGHBORHOOD HOUSES OF N. Y.

APPENDIX B

A SETTLEMENT CATECHISM [13]

BY MARY KINGSBURY SIMKHOVITCH

OF GREENWICH HOUSE

What is a Settlement?

It is a family living in a neighborhood.

What kind of a family?

A group of people who have had educational and social advantages.

What kind of a neighborhood?

A neglected neighborhood.

Why does the Settlement family choose to live in such a neighborhood?

Because it wishes to understand the problems of the wage-earner.

What does the family do?

It shares in the normal neighborhood life.

Has the family an object?

Yes; the object all families should have, namely, to take its full share in the development of the life of the community where its lot is cast.

---

[13] Originally published about ten years ago by the Association of Neighborhood Workers which was the predecessor to the present United Neighborhood Houses of New York.

190

How is this "object" realized?

Through the co-operation of the Settlement family with its neighbors.

Does the Settlement aim to "do good"?

It does not. It aims to be good with the rest of the like-minded neighbors. It aims, in co-operation with its neighbors, to work out the best sort of neighborhood life possible.

Is the Settlement a "charity"?

As the Settlement is a family, it cannot be a charity, although it may do charitable things and its efforts may be supported by charitable funds.

Is the Settlement an "institution"?

No; a Settlement is a group of persons—a family, but such a group may carry on institutional work if it is appropriate, if the community needs it.

When will it be appropriate to carry on institutional work?

When no other agency can do it as well or better.

Should the Settlement carry on institutional work permanently?

No, it should carry it on only so long as it is absolutely needed.

Why then should a Settlement begin such work?

Because by initiating such work it can prove whether it is needed and can then get others to take it over and especially in this way can develop a better organization on the part of the community itself to meet community needs.

Is the Settlement a "mission"?

No, for the purpose of a mission is to propagate a certain belief, whether that belief be religious or social.

The Settlement is not a propagandist institution. It is a family, and while it is possible that all members of a family may hold the same views—political, social or religious—it is not of the essence of a family life that it should become a propagandist group.

Should a Settlement hold public religious services?

This is the work of the Church. Why should a family usurp this function?

How does the Settlement family maintain itself?

Some members pay their own way and some are supported by friends of the family, who believe that it is valuable that a certain number of the group should give their whole time to neighborhood life, which they would be unable to do if earning their livelihood by other means.

If the Settlement is a family, what is the Settlement's Committee or Board of Managers?

Such boards are friends of the family who help it to carry on its neighborhood enterprises and give it counsel. Such a board may properly refuse to give support to any enterprise in which it does not believe or may encourage by financial help that in which it does believe.

Is such a board necessary?

It or something similar is necessary unless the Settlement family is entirely self-sustaining, and this rarely is the case.

How should such a board be made up?

It should be made up of representatives of the family which constitutes the Settlement, and friends of this family who help to carry out this work.

How can others than the board help the Settlement family carry on its work?

By joining the Settlement society from which the board is chosen or, in case there is no board, by sending contributions to the family itself.

How otherwise can people help the Settlement family carry on its work?

By assisting the residents at the Settlement.

What do "capitalists" think of Settlements?

Often they think they are "hot beds of radicalism."

What do "radicals" think of the Settlement?

Often they think the Settlement is an instrument of capitalism by which working people are lulled into inactivity.

What do "religious people" sometimes think of the Settlement?

That it must be irreligious, if it does not hold religious services or is not connected with the Church.

What do those who have studied the Settlements most closely think about them?

That they are neither "conservative" nor "radical," "religious" nor "irreligious" but that, guided by experience and life itself, they propose to build up a more valuable kind of neighborhood life than that which at present exists, irrespective of theory and regardless of criticism.

How can a neighborhood life be developed except in co-operation with city life?

It cannot. Experience gained in one district, while not identical with that of another, has elements in common with it. The neighborhood is a social municipal unit, and just as the State is dependent upon the family, so is it upon the neighborhood. Neighborliness is as primitive and as permanent as is the family. The city can never be understood nor its problems met unless the neighborhoods that make it up are known and their problems met. The work must be correlated at every turn.

Can neighborhood problems be solved apart from social problems?

They cannot. They are closely related.

Does the Settlement then claim to be a "solution" of the social problem?

It never has made such a claim, and never can, for the Settlement is a family, and the family is not a solution. Every member of the family is free to hold what "views" he or she chooses—religious or social, but each member is bound not to force his views upon the group. No member of a family has a right to tyrannize over another.

Is a Settlement a "palliative for social ills"?

Again it must be repeated it is not a palliative, nor is it conceivable that any family could be a palliative.

What is the general function of a Settlement family?

To co-operate with the neighborhood and by this means to increase the capacity for community action.

How is this co-operation brought about?

By making the Settlement house a social centre.

Why should not the school be the social centre rather than the Settlement?

The school should be a social centre for the neighborhood, with the Settlement family taking the lead in making it such; but no development of the school will ever supersede the social life that gathers about families.

Why is the Settlement family any more important than any other neighborhood family as a centre for neighborhood life?

Only because by virtue of certain advantages—education, financial or otherwise—the Settlement family is able to be neighborly in a wider and more effective way than are other families in Settlement neighborhoods.

What are the advantages of Settlement life in comparison with other kinds of social work?

1. Seeing things in relation one to another. Ordinarily the social worker's mind is fastened on one particular aspect of the social problem.

2. Giving an unparalleled opportunity to understand the indigenous life of city neighborhoods and thereby secure training for political activity.

3. By being a member of a group rather than working as an isolated individual partial views are checked up by the constant criticism of the other members of the group.

Is the Settlement permanent?

The time is not yet in sight when industrial neighborhoods will not be benefited by the presence of such a family group ever on the alert, ready to help, eager to defend and desirous of passing on to others what the group has learned. Every such neighborhood needs a Settlement.

What is the measure of efficiency of a Settlement?

The extent of its co-operation.

Is efficiency indicated by the number and character of clubs and classes and activities generally carried on in the Settlement House?

Only partially. It is indicated as well by the personnel of the Settlement group. As the Settlement's life is a family life its work is more akin to that of the artist than of the business man, and while the efficiency of the artist can perhaps be measured it is not in quantitative terms.

Is there then no common ground on which the Settlement family meets?

There is.

What is it?

The belief that co-operation on the part of all the members of the community is both desirable and possible.

How else may we define this belief?

As a belief in democracy.

Would any one who does not believe in democracy be a suitable member of a Settlement House?

He would not.

Are there any other heresies from a point of view of a Settlement?

There are not. The only heretic is he who does not believe in democracy.

APPENDIX C

THE GREAT WAR AND THE FOREIGN BORN POPULATION OF THE UNITED STATES

ENEMY ALIENS

Enemy alien males between the ages of 18 and 45 residing in the United States, were compelled by law to register between June 5, 1917, and September 12, 1918. The following table shows both the number registered and the relation by per cent to the total number of aliens in the country.

NATIONALITY	NUMBER	PER CENT
Austria-Hungary	751,212	19.38
German Empire	158,809	4.09
Turkey	81,608	2.10
Bulgaria	19,873	.52
Total Enemy Alien Males	1,011,502	26.38

Out of this number only 6,000 were interned in detention camps under Presidential warrants as being dangerous.

PARTICIPATION OF FOREIGN BORN CITIZENS

The following has been compiled from figures furnished by the Foreign Language Information Service of the American Red Cross.

197

Foreign language groups in the American Expeditionary Force:

NATIONALITY	NUMBER	KILLED
Italian	300,000	4,000
Jewish	250,000	3,500
Polish	170,000	?
Czechoslovak	125,000	2,000
Greek	60,000	?
Lithuanian	35,000	500
Jugoslav	20,000	?
Russian	20,000	?
Ukrainian	18,000	500
Hungarian	7,000	200

The War Department reports that figures for those of German birth or parentage serving in the American army are not accessible. It has been variously estimated, however, "that from 10 to 15% of the American expeditionary forces were men of German birth or origin."

The following is a partial list of contributions to the Fourth Liberty Loan by foreign language groups:

Italian	$150,000,000
Jugoslav	3,000,000
Ukrainian	1,000,000
Lithuanian	12,000,000
Hungarian	2,500,000
Russian	40,000,000

It should be noted that one-half of the Russian total was raised in New York alone. Seventy per cent of all Czechoslovaks subscribed to this loan but the figures in money are not made accessible. No estimate has been made of the Jewish contribution. Men of Greek birth or descent subscribed a total of $30,000,000 for the first four Liberty Loan drives.

APPENDIX D

DEPARTMENT OF THE INTERIOR

Bureau of Education   Circular No. 34   Washington

FOREIGN-BORN WHITES UNABLE TO SPEAK
ENGLISH, ILLITERATE, AND ATTENDING
SCHOOL IN THE UNITED STATES, CENSUS 1910

AGE LIMITS	INABILITY TO SPEAK ENGLISH	ILLITERACY	SCHOOL ATTENDANCE
10 years of age and over	2,953,011	1,650,361	446,745
15 years of age and over	2,896,606	1,637,677	138,253
21 years of age and over	2,565,612	1,507,493	35,614

APPENDIX E

FINANCIAL REPORTS AND FINANCES

In order to give a general survey of the scope of settlement finance, the following brief commentaries upon the reports of typical houses are appended:

BOYS' CLUB OF AVENUE A, N. Y.: 1913 disbursements were $28,272.00. For the year ending September 30th, 1919, disbursements totalled $63,323.00 of which approximately $23,000.00 was the payroll of the club, $12,000.00 the building maintenance and miscellaneous, and $14,725.00 for summer camp expense.

CHRISTODORA HOUSE OF N. Y.: In 1913 the total budget was $40,905.00. For the year ending October 31st, 1920, total expenses were $43,080.00. Of this, salaries amounted to $15,998.00. Miscellaneous expenses for the New York house amounted to $9,902.00. Expenses in connection with Northover Camp amounted to $12,572.00. $5,190.00 was received for board at Northover and contributions for fresh air work amounted to $5,813.00. The budget included a $1,000.00 item for the Haven's Relief Fund.

COLLEGE SETTLEMENT OF N. Y.: For the year ending Ocotber 1st, 1920, disbursements for the work in New York amounted to $11,230.00 of which $7,918.00 was for salaries. The expenses for the camp at Mt. Ivy were $8,266.00 additional.

EAST SIDE HOUSE OF N. Y.: For the year ending December 31st, 1920, expenditures were $62,201.00. Of this amount $38,555.00 was for salaries; $11,437,00 for food, materials and supplies; $2,695.00 for fuel and lighting; $4,917.00 for repairs and renewals; and $1,122.00 for assistance, loans, etc.

EDUCATIONAL ALLIANCE OF N. Y.: For the year ending December 31st, 1918, both income and expenditures are assigned to various committees. The expenses for these committees total as follows: Finance, $4,896.00; Membership, $244.00; Legal Aid Bureau, $7,347.00; Education, $13,448.00; Religious Work, $21,770.00; House, $53,-761.00; Social Work, $19,132.00; Young Peoples' Branch, $6,811.00; Approximate Total, $127,418.00.

GREENWICH HOUSE OF N. Y.: Both income and expenditures are divided among special classes of work, with a total for the year ending September 30, 1920 of $35,494.00   Other expenses totaled $40,005.00.   Included in the latter are items for administration of $19,-197.00 and general house expense of $13,615.00.   Expenses of benefits amounted to $4,273.00 from which receipts of $11,579.00 were realized.

HENRY STREET SETTLEMENT OF N. Y.: Not only is the settlement responsible for the Visiting Nurse Service for which it is famous, but it operates three branch houses in New York City besides country places. The annual report for 1920 shows expenses as follows: Social Service, $71,282.00; Of this, Administration and General accounted for, $29,862.00; Branch, Hamilton House, $7,481.00; Branch, Lincoln House, $8,637.00; Branch, 79th Street House, $8,353.00; and Country Places, $25,628.00. The Expenditures of the Visiting Nurse Service were $329,-678.00 additional.

HUDSON GUILD OF N. Y.: For the year ending September 30th, 1919, the total disbursements were $42,887.00. Of these $30,026.00 were in the general fund. Salaries formed an item of $18,422.00. Outside of the general fund the Clubs' Council expended $1,595.00 for coal, light, etc. The expenses of the Hudson Guild Library were $1,508.00. This was more than covered by dues, etc. The expenses of the Milk Station were $1,413.00; this activity also was self-supporting. $8,343.00 was expended for the Hudson Guild Farm, including repairs, maintenance and salaries.

LENNOX HILL SETTLEMENT OF N. Y.: Combined budget and housekeeping account for the year ending December 31, 1919 showed expenditures of $31,830.00. Of this amount $10,503.00 was for regular salaries; $1,858.00 for special salaries; and $2,680.00 for wages. Housekeeping expenses including service totalled $6,985.00 which was more than $1,300.00 in excess of the receipts from residents. Separate accounts were kept for the Boys' and Mens' Club, with a total expenditure of $19,493.00, and also for the Co-operative Store Fund, the Vocational Work Fund, the District Nursing Fund, and the Americanization and Arts and Crafts Fund.

MUSIC SCHOOL SETTLEMENT OF N. Y.: The report of the treasurer for the year ending December 31, 1919 shows disbursements amounting to $82,336.00; this amount included a payment of $39,796.00 to the endowment fund as well as $7,000.00 applied toward the cancellation of loans. The payroll of teachers amounted to $18,362.00; salaries including director, etc., amounted to $5,438.00; wages $1,153.00; expense accounts $5,794.00. It is noteworthy that the school receipts amounted to $13,885.00.

RICHMOND HILL HOUSE OF N. Y.: Total expenditures for the year ending April 1, 1920, amounted to $10,-370.00; salaries including janitor amounted to $3,963.00. The general expense maintenance, etc., including summer camp amounted to $2,335.00; printing, multigraphing, stationery, etc., to $1,367.00.

UNION SETTLEMENT OF N. Y.: Expenses under the general fund amounted to $16,982.00, of this salaries amounted to $1,375.00 and wages, $1,989.00. The maintenance of the club house amounted to $6,883.00. The special fund account contained seven items totalling $31,-313.00 additional; of which the two largest were House-By-the Sea $18,088.00 and summer work $7,129.00. The women's auxiliary of the settlement raised $13,062.00 and expended $8,171.00 which is in addition to the figures given above.

UNIVERSITY SETTLEMENT OF N. Y.: See comment in Chapter VIII of text.

SOUTH END HOUSE OF BOSTON: The form in which the annual reports are published makes them particularly useful to the student of social conditions. The work of the house is not only made intelligible to outsiders but accurate records are kept. These are presented in a form which gives them significance wider than the mere chronicle of what has been going on in one corner of the city of Boston. In reading over the reports one is inspired by the thought of what work equally well done may mean to the nation and to society. It is to be regretted that no budget report is published.

HULL HOUSE OF CHICAGO: At the time this goes to press no financial statement of this, the leading settlement in America, is obtainable. None has ever been filed in the Library of the Russell Sage Foundation in New York though according to the year book a quarterly report is made to the trustees and an annual report to the Subscriptions Investigating Committee of the Chicago Association of Commerce. The house is incorporated with a self-perpetuating board of seven trustees each elected for a period of seven years.

CHICAGO COMMONS: The following is from the report of 1920: "It has required a hard and continuous struggle throughout these twenty-five years to acquire the present building equipment, valued at $103,640.00 which now stands clear of all encumbrances, the purchase of the leased land having been made this last year. The upkeep and maintenance of the buildings are now provided for by the income received from the neighborhood groups using the public rooms, from the resident household for their living quarters, and from the interest on invested funds. The Leah D. Taylor Memorial Fund has been started by residents with the hope that it may eventually provide the salary of a family counsellor and neighborhood visitor. Every dollar which is now given, therefore, goes directly to the support and development of the human service rendered at Chicago Commons not only in its great cosmopolitan industrial neighborhood, but in promoting many interests vital to the city, the country, the state, and the nation."— The report then goes on to say that the average sum received annually, namely, $14,111.21, ninety-four per cent of which was contributed in amounts ranging from $1.00 to $100.00, will not suffice for rising costs and sets the goal to be raised at $20,000.

COLLEGE SETTLEMENT OF PHILADELPHIA: For the year ending September 30, 1913, the treasurer's account shows total disbursements of $15,696.00, of which $3,943.00 was to pay the salary of the Head worker and Assistants. $5,573.00 was paid over to the Head Worker for house maintenance, and $2,630.00 was collected by the headworker from board and rentals. The balance of the disbursements went toward paying taxes, interest on mortgages and rent on some of the properties occupied. The item of $2,444.00 for table board was more than covered by receipts. Janitor, house service, and cleaning amounted to $1,970.00.

KINGSLEY ASSOCIATION OF PITTSBURGH: Operates Kingsley House in the city with annual expenditure (1920) of $19,916.63, also the Lillian Home a fresh air farm at Valencia, Pa., with expenditures of $20,915.31, and Lillian Rest at Valencia a convalescent hospital with budget of $28,181.83.

TOYNBEE HALL: Administered by the Universities' Settlement in East London. The Public Account for the year ending June 30, 1914 shows a total expenditure of £1272. Of this £374 is charged to general expenditures of which sum only a little over £200 went to salaries and office expenses. For maintenance the sum of £689 was expended. This included repairs, rates and taxes, coals, gas and water, and servants' wages and board. In addition to the Public Account £428 was expended by the Education Committee and £68 by the Entertainment Committee.

BIBLIOGRAPHY

The following reference list has been compiled by way of suggestion for those who may be tempted to look further into not only the history and the aims of the social settlement but also to take up a detailed study of the larger problems of social conditions and social philosophy. It has been impossible to make the Bibliography in any way complete. The attempt has been made, however, to make it suggestive and broad in scope.

I

BIBLIOGRAPHY OF SOCIAL SETTLEMENTS

Addams, Jane: "Twenty Years at Hull House".... 1910
Barnett, Samuel A.: "University Settlements"...... 1898
Barnett, Mrs. Samuel A.: "Canon Barnett, His Life, Work, and Friends".................................. 1919
Coit, Stanton: "Neighborhood Guilds".................... 1892
Daniels, John: "America via the Neighborhood"...... 1920
Maltiens, W. H.: "The Meaning of Social Settlement Movement"...................................... 1909
Merrill Lilburn: "Winning the Boy"........................ 1908
Milner, Lord: "Reminiscence of Arnold Toynbee".. 1894
Reason, W.: "University and Social Settlement"...... 1898
Stelzle, Charles: "Boys of the Street: How to Win Them" 1904

Wald, Lillian D.: "The House on Henry Street".... **1915**

White, Gaylord S.: "Social Settlement after
    Twenty-five Years" **1911**

Woods, Robert A. and Albert J. Kennedy: "Hand-
    book of Settlements." Contains a valuable
    bibliography. **1911**

Proceedings of the National Conference of Social
    Work. ....Annual

Reports (The best file of Reports is in the Library
    of the Russell Sage Foundation, N. Y.)

Boys Club of Avenue A...................................1919, 1920

Christodora House 1912, 1913, 1914, 1920

College Settlement....................................1919, 1920

East Side House 1913, 1919, 1921

Educational Alliance......1915 (25th Anniversary), 1919

Greenwich House 1913, 1920

Grosvenor Neighborhood House 1919

Harlem House.. 1919

Henry Street Settlement
                    1913 (20th Anniversary), 1920

Hudson Guild
            1910, 1911, 1912 (25th Anniversary), 1920

Lennox Hill 1918, 1919

Madison House..1920, 1921

Music School Settlement 1919

Richmond Hill House 1920

Riis House 1920

Union Settlement 1920

University Settlement 1920

South End House of Boston 1907-1921

Hull House of Chicago, Year Books............1913-1921

Chicago Commons 1920

College Settlement of Philadelphia 1903-1913
Kingsley House of Pittsburgh 1920
Toynbee Hall ....1907-1908 to 1913-1914

II

SOCIAL CONDITIONS

Addams, Jane: "Spirit of Youth in the City Streets" 1909

Addams, Jane: "Philanthropy and Social Progress" 1899

Antin, Mary: "The Promised Land" 1912

Bierstadt, Edward H.: "Alien America" (In preparation).

Brown, William Adams: "The Church and Social Reconstruction" 1920

Butler, Fred Clayton: Community Americanization —U. S. Dept. of Interior, Bureau of Education, Bulletin 76 1920

Churchill, Winston: "The Dwelling Place of Light" (a novel) 1917

Edwards, Albert: "Comrade Yetta" (a novel) 1913

Factory Investigating Commission, State of New York, Robert F. Wagner, Chairman; Abram I. Elkus, Chief Counsel, 1st, 2nd, 3rd, 4th Reports 1912-1915

Manly, Basil M.: Commission on Industrial Relations, Report, U. S. Senate, Document No. 415, 64th Congress 1916

Parker, Carleton: "The Casual Laborer and other Essays" 1920

Riis, Jacob: "Battle with the Slum" 1902

Riis, Jacob: "How the Other Half Lives" 1890
Riis, Jacob: "Making of an American" 1912
Steiner, Edward A.: "On the Trail of the Immi-
    grant" 1906
Steiner, Edward A.: "From Alien to Citizen"...... 1914
The Survey: See Files.
Commission of Inquiry—The Interchurch World
    Movement: Report on the Steel Strike of 1919
Committee on Criminal Courts:
    Justice for the Poor 1915
    Reorganizing the Criminal Courts 1914
Publications of the Juvenile Protective Association
    of Chicago:
    The Department Store Girl 1911
    First Lessons in Gambling 1911
    Five and Ten Cent Theaters 1911
    Juvenile-Adult Offender 1912
    The Girl Employed in Hotels and Restaurants 1912
    Boys in the County Jail 1913
    A Study of Bastardy Cases 1914
    Revised Manual of Juvenile Laws 1916
    The Straight Girl on the Crooked Path................ 1916
    Public Dance Hall of Chicago 1917
    Junk Dealing and Juvenile Delinquency............. 1919
    Summary of Work 1913-1920
Report upon Illegal Practices of the United States
    Department of Justice by the National Popular
    Government League, R. S. Brown, Zachariah
    Chafee, Jr., Felix Frankfurter, Roscoe Pound,
    and others 1920
Annual Report of the Court of Special Sessions.

III

HISTORICAL, ECONOMIC AND PHILOSOPHICAL

A. E. (George W. Russell): "The National Being, Some Thoughts on Irish Polity," 1916

Adams, Thomas S. and Helen L. Summer: "Labor Problems" (especially chapter on Poverty, Earnings and Unemployment) 1914

Beard, Mary: "A Short History of American Labor Movement" 1920

Beveridge, W. H.: "Unemployment, A Problem of Industry" 1912

Burritt, A. W. and H. S. Dennison and others: "Profit Sharing, Its Principles and Practice" 1918

Cartwright, George W.: "The Mutual Interests of Labor and Capital" 1919

Commons, John R. and associates: "History of Labor in the U. S.," 2 vols. 1918

Dewey, John: "Democracy and Education, An Introduction to the Philosophy of Education".... 1917

Dewey, John and Evelyn: "Schools of To-morrow 1915

Ellwood, Charles A.: "The Social Problem"........ 1915

Ellwood, Charles A.: "An Introduction to Social Psychology" 1917

Fabian Tracts: Publications of the Fabian Society, 25 Tothill Street, Westminster, London.

Series I   General Socialism.

" II   Applications of Socialism to Particular Problems.

" III   Local Government Powers: How to use them.

" IV   General Politics and Fabian Policy.

" V   Biographical.

George, Henry: "Progress and Poverty" 1879

Gleason, Arthur: "Workers' Education, American and Foreign Experiments" 1921

Goode, Wm. T.: "Bolshevism at Work" 1920

Hammond, J. L. and Barbara: "The Town Laborer" 1917

Henderson, Arthur: "The Aims of Labor" 1918

Hunter, Robert: "Poverty" 1912

Kirkup, Thomas: "History of Socialism" 1913

Kelley, Florence: "Modern Industry" 1914

Lecky, W. E. H.: "History of European Morals" 1869

MacDonald, J. Ramsay: "The Socialist Movement" (especially chapter "What Socialism is NOT") 1911

Marot, Helen: "American Labor Unions" 1914

Marot, Helen: "Creative Impulse in Industry; a proposition for educators" 1918

Marot, Helen: "Handbook of Labor Literature" 1899

Marx, Karl: "Capital," English Translation, Edited by Engels ...., 1904

Marx, Karl, and Frederick Engels: "The Communist Manifesto" 1848

O'Brien, George: "An Essay on Medieval Economic Teaching" 1920

Penty, A. J.: "Guilds and the Social Crisis"........ 1919

Penty, A. J.: "A Guildsman's Interpretation of History" 1919

Rae, John: "Contemporary Socialism" 1889

Renard, Georges: "Guilds in the Middle Ages," Edited by G. S. H. Cole 1919

Russell, Bertrand: "Proposed Roads to Freedom" 1919

Russell, Charles Edward: "Bolshevism and the
United States" 1919

Russell, Charles Edward B.: "Problems of
Juvenile Crimes, Barnett House Papers" 1917

Simkhovitch, V. S.: "Marxism Versus Socialism" 1913

Spargo, John: "Bolshevism" 1919

Streightoff, F. H.: "Distribution of Incomes in
the U. S." 1912

Stelzle, Charles: "Church and Labor" 1910

Tannenbaum, Frank: "The Labor Movement" 1921

Toynbee, Arnold: "The Industrial Revolution of
the 18th Century in England" 1884

Wallas, Graham: "The Great Society, A Psycho-
logical Analysis" 1920

Ward, Harry F.: "The New Social Order, Princi-
ples and Programs 1919

Ward, Harry F.: "Social Evangelism".................... 1915

Ward, Lester F.: "Pure Sociology, A Treatise
on the origin and spontaneous development
of society" 1914

Webb, Beatrice and Sidney: "Industrial Democracy" (especially chapter "Economic Charac-
teristics") 1914

Wells, H. G.: "Russia under the Shadows".......... 1921

Williams, Aneurin: "Co-partnership and Profit-
sharing" 1913

Statistical Atlas of U. S., Dept. of Interior, Bureau
of Census 1914